I Identification: Human and Divine

The Annie Kinkead Warfield Lectures, 1962–1963

Kenneth Joseph Foreman

Identification:
HUMAN
and
DIVINE

JOHN KNOX PRESS | *Richmond, Virginia*

Library of Congress Catalog Card Number: 63-9002

J.8816

IN BEATAM MEMORIAM UXORIS MEAE
QUAE MECUM SAEPE IN HIS AULIS
SEDEBAT

I *Foreword*

The six chapters of this book consist essentially of the six lectures with this name and content which were given as the Annie Kinkead Warfield Lectures at Princeton Theological Seminary, Princeton, New Jersey, November 12-16, 1962.

My thanks are hereby cordially expressed to the trustees of the Lectureship for their confidence in extending the invitation to deliver these lectures, as well as to those who listened, for their Christian patience.

Grateful public acknowledgment is offered to those who helped further this project in various ways, especially the library staffs of the Louisville Presbyterian, Union at Richmond, Colgate-Rochester, and other seminaries; to Mrs. Grace L. Cosby for typing the final draft, and Miss Mary Virginia Robinson of John Knox Press for correcting many of my errors and for careful shepherding of the manuscript through the press.

Thankful remembrance also includes my professors in college, seminary, and graduate school who taught me respect for Christian scholarship and scholarly Christians. Not least eminent among these was Dr. Benjamin Breckinridge Warfield himself, founder of this Lectureship, whose prodigious scholarship and unique brilliance as a teacher made his classes memorable.

If I am found to have deviated at any point from positions taken by any who taught me, it is understood in such matters that exceptions are taken to ideas, not persons. I have often learned most from those with whom I most sincerely differed.

As for the history of these lectures, the germ was a one-period lecture given in a summer session at Louisville Presbyterian Theological Seminary. By an irresistible process known to all professors, this expanded first to two and then to three lectures, the three being given at Union Theological Seminary in Richmond, Virginia, in 1955. These later were broken up and broken down, changed and more than doubled in length (the increase, I hope, being in content and not only in size), and are now essentially new.

K. J. F.

Richmond, Virginia
November 1962

 *Contents*

1. I *Make-Believe,* Human and Divine

Underneath all great truths widely and commonly accepted are many presuppositions, by which is meant truths taken for granted, truths that seem axiomatic, as well as presuppositions which are negative.

Some of these presuppositions are positive, accepted as axioms needing no proof, not usually examined, perhaps seldom recognized. Those who hold them may not be aware of their existence; they are woven into the thinker's mind, they are part of the tools of his thought. If you said to one who holds such a presupposition, "But you are assuming so and so," he would perhaps look startled, but he would say, "Of course. How could I or any sane man think otherwise?" On the other hand are negative presuppositions—what may be called, for short, unthinkables. These are ideas, solutions, propositions, from which the thinker's mind recoils as it were by instinct. Logically he may be aware that such unthinkable propositions might be entertained, but he honestly cannot see how. The thought no sooner occurs to his mind than he reacts against it. (Incidentally, one great reason for human quarrels, on a small scale or a large, is that the debaters on one side have a different set of unthinkables from those on the other.)

Negative and positive presuppositions alike are usually unexamined. The thinker is so busy carving out his dogma on the rocky cliff of Reality that he scarcely notices the scaffold on which he swings. Yet if the positive presuppositions are not true, the scaffold will not hold, the dogma fails; if the presuppositions are not true, the dogma is not likely to be true. If the unthinkable proposition turns out to be true after all, then again the doctrine, being baseless, will fall.

The intention of this study is to examine one of the most vital presuppositions of theology and of life: *Identification.* It is rather more than a principle, though it is that. It stands in its own right, and calls for explicit recognition and analysis. There is nothing especially novel about this. Everyone would admit that the presupposition is true; many will have thought of it before. If the approach taken seems to be indirect, the reason will appear as we proceed. First of all, we take a look at the background, namely, Make-believe, human and divine.

God is not a liar. He is the God of truth. Yet his revelation contains some elements which, in a strictly literal sense, cannot be called true. I do not refer to parts of the Bible like the ending of the 137th Psalm, nor to statements made by Job's friends or by that ambiguous cynic called Ecclesiastes. I am not referring to partial revelations to be superseded when that which is perfect is come. This has nothing to do, for the moment, with alleged mythical or mythological elements in Scripture. I mean that in the heart of the revelation there are embedded propositions, explicit or implied, dealing with God himself and with his will, as the Westminster Confession puts it (Chapter I), which as a literalist counts truth are not true, and yet seen in a larger light may turn out to be most profoundly true.

At this point, at least a measure of clarity is desirable about concepts with which we shall be working, and which are notoriously controversial. It was a comfort to me once to hear a great teacher say that every speaker or writer has the right to use any word, or to coin a word if he can find none ready-made to his purpose, in any sense he wishes, *provided* (a) he lets his audience or his readers know, to begin with, what he intends by the word, and (b) always uses it consistently; (c) provided also that he does not invite confusion by violating common usage. For instance, a chef in giving out a certain recipe may say, "When I say pan, I mean an electric frying pan." That is legitimate. But if he says, "When I mean an electric frying pan, sometimes I shall use the words powder puff," that is not legitimate, for his substitute word, his key word, is not only arbitrary but has a definite normal meaning which has no connection with the word for which it is a substitute.

At any rate, I shall take advantage of the alleged privilege. Since we may be using pretty slippery words capable of being understood in many ways, we should at least be clear about what our big words mean.

We have used three of these already: presupposition, revelation, and truth. Enough has been said about presuppositions for the present. As to *revelation*, on the running dispute between those who hold to a "propositional" theory of revelation and those who hold that revelation is personal, I take it that both are true but neither is exclusively true. Granted that the Confession of Faith, and most contemporary Protestant theologians, are right in making God's revelation of himself and his will the central feature; yet person and proposition can seldom be neatly distinguished. The sentence, "GOD IS LOVE," is on the one hand a proposition, however vague it may appear to be. Yet, taken seriously, it is also a revelation of the nature and the will—indeed, the nature of the will—of God. On the other hand, while God's supreme revelation of himself is not in propositions but in a Person, the fact remains that we have to have propositions to express what we mean by the Person's nature and functions and relationships. Christology of any type simply bristles with propositions. Thus the movement is reciprocal: personal revelation implies propositions, and propositional revelation on any vital level is a revealing of the purpose of God, the kind of God God is. If now and then I seem to be leaning to the side of propositional revelation, that is only an illusion, caused by the use of the word *truth*. (Of which more presently.)

The word truth can refer, and usually does, to propositions; but it can refer to persons. Admitted, the word "truth" is sometimes used in ridiculously inappropriate connections. Men on billboards talk about the "honest taste" of a certain cigarette. But a taste is neither honest nor dishonest, it is what it is. Only a *person* can be a hypocrite; we can speak meaningfully of false persons. So likewise, if I seem to be defining truth in a way appropriate to propositions, let it be understood that it can apply to persons also. As to what constitutes revelation, it is the will of God as directed to our mental and/or other response. The content of revelation is what, or whom, God wants us to know. The "how" of revelation, the method by which God causes us to know what he wants us to know, lies outside our present inquiry, and probably outside all our possible finding out. As to the channel or channels of revelation, while I believe with the Confession of Faith that there are other channels besides the Bible, in these chapters I shall be referring to the Biblical revelation, so that this particular point is not an essential one for our purpose.

Now, what is *truth?* Defining it, or offering theories about its criteria, is a tricky business, and highly controversial. All theories of truth have their weaknesses. For the purposes of our discussion we shall assume the correspondence theory of truth.[1] It has the advantage of being what most normal people do think truth is, even if they never formulated the theory or even heard of it. On this theory, truth is a quality of propositions. Nonsense cannot be true or false, because nonsense is not propositional except in bare form. For a proper proposition there has to be a subject, a predicate, and some relating-word between them, some connecting link. The cat is on the fence. The apple is sweet. The book is inaccurate. The watch is 37 seconds fast. Now most ordinary propositions in everyday life (like these) can be verified directly or indirectly. If the cat is not on the fence, assuming it to be clear to all concerned, to what "the" cat and "the" fence refer, then the original proposition is false.

By verification we mean: By observation or otherwise we check the proposition with the facts to which it refers. If the facts are related as the proposition relates them, then the proposition is true, because it *corresponds* with the facts. This is no place to go into all the ramifications of the theory. For instance, in one or two of the examples given, the expressed relation is not between two objects but between an object and a quality. Is "The apple is sweet" true or false? Is this quality actually inherent in the object as alleged? That proposition would be proved to be false if the fruit were not an apple but an orange; or if the apple were not sweet at all. If there is no such situation, or a very different situation from that described in the proposition, then the proposition is false.

It will be objected, and it is objected, that the correspondence theory of truth does not help us with unverifiable propositions, or "facts" which cannot be agreed on publicly as can cat, apple, and sweet. Following this objection, certain philosophers have made it appear that all religious or indeed metaphysical propositions are without meaning.[2]

Now some propositions are vague because the terms are not clear. For instance: "This room is stuffy." Is that true or false? It might be true for some, not for others. But the proposition could be made definite by agreeing on some specific criterion for "stuffy," e.g., "containing such and such a percentage of carbon dioxide." Far more important, of course, are propositions dealing with values, with intangibles, and with the high realities pointed to in religious language. Let it be granted that in such realms we speak beyond our knowledge, as Kant pointed out, and that anything we say points in the direction of reality rather than describing it precisely. Nevertheless, the standpoint taken here is that religious propositions refer by intention to facts and relations not subject to direct observation, and yet believed to be real. It is of no use to say that "God is love" is a meaningless sentence so long as "God is not love" is perceived to be a direct contradiction. The speaker or writer of such a proposition believes there is a correspondence between his words and reality, however inaccessible the reality may presently be to total demonstration.

All this is sobersided enough. Where we run into difficulty is in the realm of the imagination, the realm of make-believe. Imagination deals with facts in a way different from that of logical analysis, a way all its own. Imagination may not deal with facts at all. Shakespeare's *Tempest* is one of innumerable examples.

No one wants to know the latitude and longitude of that famous island; no one cares very much whether it could be proved that there is not any situation anywhere now, and never was, corresponding to the lush poetry of Shakespeare. The playwright had the genius not only to create a world, but, what may be more difficult, to insert fictional events into history. Viewed as a historian, Shakespeare was a liar when he wrote *The Tempest*, and a liar when he wrote *Henry V*. But nobody calls him a liar for this. To be sure, he would be a dangerous liar to a ship's captain who might try to find Prospero's island by the poet's directions, and a misleading liar to a man trying to ascertain precisely what King Henry V said to his troops at a particular moment in history. Nevertheless, the poet's imagination is such as meets the approval of those who can enter into it for what it is worth.

However, our interest is not in literary imagination but in imagination as a universal human capacity and practice, and even habit.

Imagination is ethically neither bad nor good in itself. Yet it involves something which is universally regarded as bad: namely, making, explicitly or implicitly, propositions which are known to the speaker or thinker of them *not* to correspond with reality, and yet in a way are different from a lie.

It is a somewhat complex attitude of mind. A simple illustration can be taken from the life of a child, the first time my own child gave evidence of the possession of imagination. He was not showing off at the time; he was talking to himself, unaware of being observed. He walked up a stairway holding a small stick upright in his hand, saying, "Brella." Now he knew the stick was not an umbrella. Implicit in his mind lay the proposition: This is not an umbrella; and its corollary: This stick will not keep off rain or sunshine. But also in his mind lay a shadowy second proposition: This stick IS an umbrella; and its corollary: This umbrella will keep off rain and sunshine. He knew the first propositions were true, literally; he knew the second set were false. If it had started to rain he would hardly have made believe he was dry. Yet he chose the second proposition, known not to correspond with the facts, as if it were true; indeed, he was capable of concentrating on the imagined reality as if it were the genuine reality.

Imagination always has this dual quality: a double awareness, both of a proposition which corresponds to fact, and another which is not and is not thought to be in line with objective fact. To be sure, the mind engaging in imaginative thought is not invariably aware of what the true-to-fact proposition is. A child comes on a large hole in the ground, and calls it a lion's den. He may not know what the hole really is, and doesn't care. It's more fun to call it a lion's den. A public prosecutor, "reconstructing" a crime, may not know what the actual facts were and may wish he knew. But his business requires him to use his imagination where the facts are not available. The honest prosecutor is always more or less aware of the difference between phases of the reconstruction where he knows that the story and the facts do correspond, and those phases where he has only a story and a hope that the actualities were something like it.

Both of these modes of imagination—namely, where the literally true propositions are known, and where they are not known—differ from a lie. In a lie, also, the true-to-fact propositions are known, but false-to-facts propositions are substituted for ulterior reasons. A lie is a false statement uttered or expressed knowingly, in the hope of eliciting credence. An imaginative statement also is a false statement, literally false, expressed knowingly; but there is no intention of winning believers. To put it vulgarly, the liar is fishing for suckers, the man of fancy is not.

A lie is a proposition known to the lie-maker as not corresponding to reality, and told for selfish or malicious purposes. "Sin has many tools, but a lie is the handle that fits them all," is an old proverb apposite here. A lie is seldom told for fun. It is usually a means to some bad end. It is designed to hurt or hinder someone, or to give the liar an advantage he would not otherwise have. It is told with the hope that the hearer will take it for the truth. Imagination, on the other hand, is not passed off as truth. It is not intended with malice, nor for the purpose of self-aggrandizement. It is not the handle to something sinister. It stands in its own right. A lie is both like, and different from, imaginative statements. In both cases the speaker knows the difference between the statement and the facts; but the liar hopes the respondent will not be aware of this gap, while the practicer of imagination does not really care whether the respondent does or does not take his fancy for literal truth. Indeed, he may take great pains to keep the respondent from forgetting that the propositions are *not* literally true.

The same proposition can be told as a lie, and as imaginative language. The best example, perhaps, is Santa Claus. Children can be told the Santa Claus legend in such a way as to cause violent disillusionment when the truth is discovered, and a strong subsequent distrust of the parents whose lie has been found out. Or it can be told (as it was to this writer) in such a way as to be understood as a make-believe, a happy make-believe which can be carried on by the imaginative child long after the disillusioned one-time believer has become an infant cynic.

Imagination itself, however, is not necessarily good. It can be idle daydreaming; it can be indulged in carelessly till the subject scarcely knows the difference between fancy and fact. It may intrude where facts are called for. It may be taken up by malice, as when one invents bad motives for another's acts. However, granting all this, it is still true that imagination is not only a common ability and practice of mankind, it is in many ways beneficial and even necessary.

Imagination may or may not be an exercise of the will. If a playwright sets out to write a play, he is deliberately exercising imagination; but the habit of imaginative thinking can grow on one until literal truth comes less readily to mind than the reconstruction of fancy. This also may not be always bad. Persons who customarily speak in metaphors, and the effectiveness of metaphors themselves, give evidence that many minds, left to themselves, naturally turn to fancy. This is not invariably bad. Someone once complained of Woodrow Wilson that he preferred to see reality through the clouded glass of poetic metaphors than in the clear light of logical analysis. Perhaps the same critic would complain that our Lord saw truth through the cloudy frame of parables. Certainly if you remove from the Gospels all that has any tinge of fancy about it, you will have a sorry remnant left. All I wish to press here is that the habit of using the imagination, letting it play on the facts and the situations of life, is not necessarily bad. To be sure, fancy can be resorted to as an escape, indulged in like a drug. The end of this road, of course, is madness. But we are speaking of the more normal, and at least potentially beneficial, aspects of imagination.

In ordinary life imagination is essential. Without it there can be no planning. The chess player sees the board as it is; he also sees the board as it might look, or would look, after such and such plays. The more extensive his powers of imagination, the better he is as a chess player, other things being equal. The same thing is true of all occupations to some degree. The image of what is desired must be seen with clarity, otherwise it has no force. Men fail in ambition for lack of imagination when they see only what is and not what might be. The ideal, in any occupation or activity, is an imagined reality; the facts do not now correspond to it. But the constructive imagination not only sees what may be, it stimulates steps to the end that what may be, shall be. "Where there is no vision, the people perish." The heroes of Hebrews 11 might well be called heroes of imagination.

Imagination is necessary not only for planning the future, not only on the horizontal plane, as it were, in human affairs. It is indispensable to one trying to think of what cannot be thought. There are propositions about God which we are reasonably sure cannot be literally true, but we use them knowingly, being aware that we *must* use the language of poetry, of metaphor, of the imagination, or else be silent. When we speak of God, we are not speaking of an object which can be checked like the facts in a chemist's analysis. God is not subject to verification in the simple sense, although God can be verified in such ways as are appropriate to the apprehension of the Infinite by the finite.

Where God is concerned, we are in the position already

mentioned, where we indulge in conscious make-believe, knowing or feeling sure that our statements do not correspond to fact, and yet unable to say just what statements *would* correspond. (Probably no human language could possibly be adequate.) Yet here the situation is unique. We believe—at any rate, I believe—that it is not a case of the facts being just around the corner, so to speak, not known now but to be known. On the contrary, we are dealing with what is transcendent, incapable of being known directly, fully, and without remainder, by finite minds.[3] We are not a prosecutor building up a hypothetical case because the key witness is in Ecuador. One day he expects to get that witness and make him talk, and then the case may be a little different from what it now seems to be; but it will be a true case. The final, ultimate, most intimate truths about God can never be known and will never be known in literal completeness, except to God. We use imagination in thinking about him, not provisionally or temporarily, for lack of something better, but because such thinking is and always will be the only way we *can* think of him.[4] This is the value in all the talk about myth in the Bible. It has made us face the necessity of such modes of thinking, and made us perhaps more humble when we attempt to speak of God. This is what Calvin means by speaking of God's revelation as "accommodation";[5] what Tillich means when he says that the only non-symbolic proposition we can make about God is that all such propositions are symbolic;[6] what Brunner means when he says, speaking of certain Bible stories, that these may be myths but they are myths of revelation;[7] they are the story God wants us to tell; it is what Austin Farrer means when he talks of inspired images.[8] If we believe in the reality of revelation in the Scripture, we have the sufficient validation of the imagination, as applied to God. Symbol, myth, metaphor, are different types of imaginative outreach. Like Jacob's ladder, they may be clumsy to look at but angels can use them.

We shall return to this aspect of the use of imagination later on, as of the utmost importance.[9] Meanwhile we may note the role of imagination in interpersonal ethics and personal as well. Imagination here can be good or bad. It can inspire much evil. What is pride but thinking more highly of oneself than one ought to think? The story of the sin of man begins with the imagination. How would it feel to be as God? Imagination lent splendor to the prospect—not the last time the wine has looked brighter than the taste it left behind. What is coveting but imagining that Naboth's vineyard looks better than all the king's vineyards? How does adultery begin but in the imagination? Indeed, imagination is the door to all sins, because sin at base is idolatrous self-satisfaction and self-conceit, an illusion of wisdom greater than God's, of power greater than Satan's. Sin is made possible by the self-deceptive fancy that I am qualified to be my own lawgiver and to live up to my own standards. The very toughness of imaginative power, so valuable when applied to good ends, is the source of perpetual frustration, for the dream of the super-self survives any number of rude awakenings.

On the other hand, imagination can and does inspire much good. Parents or teachers, seeing extraordinary qualities and capacities in an ordinary boy; a woman's stubborn idealization of a less than ideal husband; St. Paul's assurance to weak and stupid converts that they did not really need any advice from him since they already possessed love and wisdom in abundance (e.g., 1 Thessalonians 1:8; 4:9; 5:1)—these and many other examples can be remembered or observed every day.

Imagination can be linked with past, present, and future. As memory, it holds the past close to us; that which cannot return returns, the past is brought back from the dead.[10] It is memory that keeps life whole; without it, the past would drop into nothingness, moment by moment, and the present arrive without context, cause, or meaning. Yet memory is nothing but imagination applied to the past. Applied to the present, imagination can have a transforming power. I cite two examples. One is the well-known experience of Hudson Taylor, who thought it quite possible that the Lord would come at any moment, and of course would visit his home among the first. How would Jesus react to Taylor's library? Thinking about that, Taylor revised his entire library, destroying some books, giving away others, setting to work to read others long neglected. The imagination told a false story, but it came out for the man's good. There was a woman in a preacher's congregation who welcomed visits from her minister, but there was one chair she would not let him use. "That's the Lord's chair," she said. "He comes and he talks with me and the work is easy." There are psychiatrists who would call that sheer delusion; others more kindly might call it a kind of parody of spiritual truth; in any case it is probably true that if that woman's mental picture of Jesus could be objectified, it would not look like the actual Jesus of Galilee. But my point is that false though the picture might be, it transformed life for a plain woman—and it transformed the woman. As a matter of fact, suppose on any Sunday, in church, every mental picture of our Lord held by the worshipers should become objectified in time and space—every face and form of Christ that now live in our private minds—what a heterogeneous collection it would be! Not all those imagined Christs could be like the true one; yet perhaps some of the phantoms farthest from "objective" reality might be a means whereby Christ best works his ageless miracle. So imagination in the form of memory may preserve the past, in the form of faith may transfigure the present, and in the form of hope may create a future. All this might not need saying, except that when later on I shall be claiming a good deal for identification, if any-one wishes to think of it as in some aspects a phenomenon of the imagination, it should not be written off merely on that account. The human race would lose its humanity if it lost its imagination. To say, "That's only imagination," indicates an unimaginative view of what imagination is.

In two particular ways imagination plays a valuable part in Christian ethics. One is the apparently simple Golden Rule. We shall return to this point; suffice it here to say that it is impos-sible to practice the Golden Rule so that it makes sense without using the imagination. The other is the strange, and from one point of view inexplicable, act and attitude of forgiveness. It is generally agreed that forgiving without forgetting is cold forgiveness. But forgiving and forgetting together involve the use of the imagination.

When an offense has been committed, an injury done, the injured person can say one of three things. Either: (a) After all, it was not an offense, or (b) I am going to forget it, or (c) I intend to act as if I had forgotten it. In any case, the imagination plays a powerful role. If I say it was not an offense, I am saying what I do not believe, for if it was an offense at the time, then my denying it now does not erase the fact. Imagination enables me to make a statement out of line with the facts as they were at the time. But suppose the offended person says: At the time of the act in question, I regarded it as an offense. Now, remembering the act clearly, I have a different reaction to it; I no longer regard it as offense, whether I did so formerly or not. This is not forgiveness but condonation. Condonation is a change of attitude regarding an act, or series of actions; whereas forgiveness, without canceling the attitude toward the act, involves a change in attitude toward the doer of the act.

Coming back then to forgiveness: if I choose to forget the whole thing, then by imagination I erase something out of the remembered past, I crush down the remembered past and substitute a different one, known to be different. If again I act as if I had forgotten it when I have not, then I am acting out a part I know to be false; in still another way I am remodeling past and present to what I choose it to have been, not what it was. Life cannot go on without forgiveness between man and man; yet forgiveness implies and includes the boldest kind of make-believe. Another solution of the problem may emerge later on; but however you look at it, forgiveness is a very strange thing, and not to be engaged in by one who is determined to think nothing that the bare facts do not support.

Now it is time to ask a crucial question. Is there anything in God corresponding to make-believe in man? Is this power of the imagination, this reconstruction of reality, attempted even if not accomplished—is this an aspect of the image of God in man? If and as we grow into the measure of the stature of the fullness of

Christ, does imagination fade away and do we see life with increasing factual precision and clarity? Is the God of truth by his very nature incapable of make-believe in any form, or is there something in him which is mirrored in and by our human gift of imagination?

First let it be admitted, as the great theologians do admit, that however firmly and happily we may believe in revelation, however true it is that to some extent we share the mind of God, still we cannot get on the inside of God's mind so as to know what he knows in the way he knows it. This is a different sort of thing from what is meant by saying—which is also true—that we cannot get on the inside of our neighbor's mind to know what *he* knows in the way he knows it. Being human like our neighbor, our mode of knowing is like his. What we lack of sharing his mind is due to our different heredity, temperament, and experience, and our consequently different attitudes. But still we sometimes must attempt to put ourselves in his place and to think as we have reason to believe he thinks. But the central reason why we cannot think as God thinks is not that our experiences and so on are different. We are creatures, not Creator; we are finite, not infinite. (To say nothing of sin.) Whatever we know, we know only in a few aspects; God's knowledge of the simplest things—a dust mote, an electron, a thought that comes and goes in a small fraction of a microsecond—is total knowledge, and what this is we cannot imagine. Whatever our neighbor knows, he knows with our kind of mind; whatever God knows, he knows with a radically different kind of mind, so radically different that some have questioned whether we should use the term "mind" in reference to it at all.

Nevertheless, we do have what we take to be a revelation. To use very plain language, God does want us to know what he thinks; he even bids us share his mind and thought. We dare to assume that while God does not reveal his whole mind to his creatures, what he does reveal is consistent with his whole mind. God-revealed and God-concealed are not, we believe, at odds.[11]

Granted all this, our question still stands: Is there any process or state of the divine consciousness which corresponds to the human quality of imagination? There can be no doubt that God approves of *our* using imagination, otherwise the Biblical revelation as we have it would be largely worthless. The question is: Is this a thought-mode made necessary for finite minds by the fact that they *are* finite, or is it in any way inherent in the infinite mind of God?

We must speak in utmost humility and by faith. Of some truths we may be reasonably sure. God does not think lies. He does not intend deceit. We may misunderstand him, but he does not set about to be misunderstood. Whatever some contributors to the Old Testament may have thought,[12] this kind of dishonest make-believe is at a polar distance from the character of God. Indeed, a being capable of lies would be something other than God, whatever transcendent attributes might be true of him.

Further, God does not think innocent falsehoods, after the manner of a child crying for the moon or a greyhound pursuing a mechanical rabbit. Most human thinking is composed of innocent falsehoods, so partial and incomplete is the best knowledge and wisdom of man. But God, who knows everything as it is and in all relationships possible and actual, is not a kind of cosmic innocent.

Certainly God does not think hypothetically, as a detective does, or a scientist. A hypothesis is a common form of our thinking every day. As we all know, it is a proposition which is believed, after a fashion; not in a direct way but indirectly. It is a proposition held tentatively, a proposition invented so as to account for other propositions known to be true.

Hypothetical thinking is a necessary and valuable aspect of our existence. Such thinking is an exercise of the imagination, with the specific purpose of removing our ignorance on some point or points, substituting reasonable probability or certainty for uncertainty, positive belief for tentative.

God, we may say, has no need for such thinking. One single fact completely contrary to a hypothesis, one known fact which could not be a fact if the hypothesis were true, is enough to destroy the hypothesis. But God knows all the facts. We believe the perfection of his nature excludes ignorance. God's knowledge of the future is another question. Most affirm for him a total knowledge of the future in minutest detail. Others affirm that he knows all the future there (now) is.[13] We are speaking of his knowledge of existing facts, past or present. To suppose that God seeks to fill up gaps in his knowledge is possible for primitive man, but hardly for the thoughtful contemporary Christian.

Another very common use of the imagination, helpful to man, surely offers no help to God. Here are included myths, metaphors, symbols, and the like. They are part of the revelation but they must be regarded as educative, they are part of God's intention to make us understand, they make truth more clear to us, or if not more clear, then more credible. But God does not need to have truth made more clear or more credible. Illustrative or pointing devices, suggesting rather than describing reality, are indeed necessary for finite minds. Only believers in a finite God could suppose that he needs such pedagogical aids. God's problem, if we may use such language, is not knowledge, it is communication. To what shall I liken the Kingdom of God? Jesus asked. No one has suggested that Jesus himself held hazy notions about the Kingdom, yet even Jesus found it difficult to dispel the haze in others' minds.

All this seems obvious enough. Up to this point we can say that make-believe, properly guarded, is not only permissible but necessary and beneficial to man; it is appropriate to his situation in finitude. But make-believe is not proper to God, he does not require it. Indeed it would seem to be no blasphemy to assert that he is incapable of it.

On the other hand, one surely real and justifiable act of imagination on God's part is to be seen in his *purposes*. This involves two very difficult problems, that of God's decrees as we call them, and that of God's relation to time. There have been those in the Reformed family who were so imbued with the idea that what God purposes, *is*, that they could not see Kant's distinction between the universe as contemplated in God's mind and the universe in being, here and running. On their view, God's relation to a nonexistent universe, or more precisely his relation to this universe nonexistent, is the same as his relation to this universe existent. In other words, it makes no difference to the timeless and impassible God whether the universe does or does not exist. Most Christians cannot go this far, and I cannot. What can be said for all, however, is that the actual future (call it so much of a future as a second can comprise, or call it the entire future of all the galaxies including those unborn)—in other words, *the* future as God purposes it—has a kind of solidity which it does not have as I envisage it. My imagined future may not come to pass at all. God's future, if it be one which he contemplates as to be actualized, does have solidity, for it will be. I am not saying this solves the problem—only that it is easily possible to think of God as holding long thoughts about the future when that time has not yet come to pass.

This leads to the other difficulty, that with time. If it is true, as the tradition has it, that to God there is no past, present, or future, but only an eternal Now, then indeed it is true that God can contemplate only what (to him) *is*, and there is no difference between the universe imagined and the universe actual, because it is only the universe actual that he imagines. But if time be real to God, or if it be conceded that at least on the time-line we can speak of God's purposes as involving the future, then we may speak with some truth of God's imagination. The very notion of plan (as we noted with human beings) involves imagination; there may well be something corresponding to it in God. "In thy book were written, every one of them, the days that were formed for me, when as yet there was none of them" (Psalm 139:16). What is this but the divine imagination?

The situation is more difficult to analyze when we think of that problem already seen to involve make-believe on the human level, i.e., *forgiveness*. Is God's forgiveness a make-believe? We saw that a human being engaging in the act or attitude of forgiveness is involved in a three-way dilemma (a trilemma) as regards truth in the strict sense we have underlined—correspondence with actual facts and their relations. The forgiver (we recall) can say: After all, it was no offense; or, I intend to forget the whole thing; or, I am going to act as if I had forgotten it. Each of these ways of dealing with an offense involves a make-believe. How does this apply to God?

We all agree that the divine forgiveness is what matters, that the divine is the only true forgiveness, in contrast with our halfway and hesitating attempts to achieve it. Is God shut up to the kind of dilemma that we encounter? God cannot say, It was no offense. The Bible is filled with the divine forgiveness, yet from cover to cover there is nothing like condonation on God's part. The reality of the offense of sin is never minimized. Whatever else may be involved, the pretense that sin is not sin is the devil's make-believe, or ours, not God's. Can God say, I am going to forget the whole thing? This would certainly involve him in a make-believe like that of the human forgiver, namely, an imaginative reconstruction of the past which omits the fatal point. It would imply that God either does not know, or pretends not to know, what he does know. Or can God say, I am going to act as if I had forgotten? Again he would be reconstructing the past; he would not be erasing a fact, as in the second way, but he would be adding a fact—i.e., an imagined fact—to the real past. For the real past does not include forgetfulness on his part, whereas to act as if he had forgotten does imaginatively claim a forgetting which did not, in fact, take place.

If the mind recoils from these possibilities as unthinkable, there is another possibility, not open to us but perhaps open to God. I say perhaps, because some would deny that God has this option; it would involve denial by him of his own perceived truth. However, by some who have toyed with the idea, God's "Lordship over time" (Brunner's expression) is said to be such that he can, at will, alter the past, i.e., change its order, its content. This is certainly not open to us; is it open to God? (This possibility if accepted is the same as the third horn of the trilemma, except that here God is conceived as having by virtue of his power as Creator, the right and power to alter the content, sequence, and events of past time.) Now the metaphysical status of past time is a difficult question indeed. But it is surely hazardous to affirm that God can alter it at will. The main reasons for supposing that he can do so are first the pressure of the alternatives just mentioned, and also the assumption that if God can create *ex nihilo*, he can (as it were) discreate *in nihil*.

This supposition assumes God's power to alter the already actualized past, and so escapes some of the previous difficulty; but it runs into another serious one. Let us call the past, as it truly was, Past A. Let us call the past God wills, after the events, Past W. If he is able to substitute Past W for Past A, we have a curious situation. I can remember Past A, because that is what I lived through. But God cannot now remember it because to him it has been annihilated. What he remembers is the past as he wills it to have been. Yet the difficulty is greater than this. Every event, if it has any effect, has an effect reaching into the future. The present is what it is, and as it is, because of the past. We cannot trace all the connections, but we cannot doubt the fact. Now suppose God does have the power, and exercises it, of annihilating the past and substituting another past in which my sins did not occur. Does he, or does he not, erase also the *effects* of my sins? If he does not, then what good does forgiveness do? (For one of the effects of sin is a hardening of the heart.) If on the other hand he does erase the effects of my sins, this involves altering the present also from being what it is. If God does this, it involves him in make-believe after all, on an immense, one may almost say infinite, scale. For in reversing, altering, or abolishing the actual past and making it by an act of will non-actual— whether the substituted past be the same only with holes in it, or a quite different texture—God would be doing violence to the basic structure of his own creation, namely, time itself. The nature of time is that it is fluid, the future flows from the present and the present from the past, and this suggested power of God to annihilate the past would mean that the actual present flows from—nothing.

I have said as much as I have, not in order to be confusing, but to point out what everyone who thinks about it discovers, that it is hard to avoid the conclusion that God himself engages in make-believe, especially at the crucial point of forgiveness. If it be argued that the divine make-believe can be justified because God can think and do whatever he wills, one must reply that the divine omnipotence never has seriously been thought to mean that God can do anything that a playful logician can suggest. Furthermore, one must press the point that for God to act as if he did not know what he does know, or as if what has happened has not happened, involves a self-contradiction which is out of harmony with what the Christian understands God to be.

This may seem far from our main problem, but it is not. We shall return to it again, with a clue that may lead us out of the difficulty here. Meanwhile, two remarks:

It is no wonder that Hinduism and Buddhism cling so tenaciously to the doctrine of Karma. Karma is the precise negation of the possibility of forgiveness. The pious Hindu or Buddhist feels that forgiveness is not only too easy, it ignores the nature of things. What's done can never be undone, it can only be balanced by suffering. (Yet the problem of sin and evil remains; the doctrine of Karma does not solve but only intensifies the tragedy of personal sin.) The other remark: It may be, as we proceed, that we shall find in the principle of identification the clue to the problem of how God can engage in make-believe without ceasing to be God. The Christian church, or certainly the Reformed family, has always stood by one seemingly crabbed proposition: That God cannot "simply forgive." The apparently complex way in which the New Testament affirms his forgiveness is not an artificial construct devised to keep theology esoteric, but is rather an indication of the only way God can forgive without ceasing to be the God of truth.

2. I *Identity* and *Identification*

The first chapter concerned a problem which might seem to be remote from our main theme of identification, namely, Make-believe, human and divine. This was partly by way of hedging against future difficulties. If it should be charged that identification is a species of make-believe, such a charge, whether well founded or not, does not destroy the value of the principle. It would only set it in the wide realm of the imagination, in the creative side of the nature of God and man.

Now we approach the principle of identification more directly. But first we have to disentangle it from identity. The latter has received extensive notice from psychologists, though as one of them said to me when I sought for light on the word, "It depends on which psychologist you ask."[1]

Without benefit of technical psychology, let us venture a few layman's thoughts. At least I can invoke the privilege mentioned in the first chapter, of explaining what I mean when I use a word.[2]

In the first place, identity is not the equivalent of identification. Identity might be called formally the meaning of A is A, or A is not non-A, whichever you prefer. Identification provisionally might be called formally the meaning of A both is and is not A; A is A and also B. If this seems logically offensive, it will be seen to be psychologically inevitable.

While identity and identification are not the same principle, yet without identity there can be no identification. The problem of identity is: Who am I? One might even ask a prior question:

AM I? The quest for identity and the quest for identification are interlinked always. Sometimes, as we shall see, the first question is answered, for many persons, sufficiently by the second. Without trying to follow step by step the sometimes agonizing pilgrimage of those who find identity a problem, we may note some of the conclusions reached by anyone who has achieved identity, at least in his own mind. First, I *am*. I am not a dream, I cannot escape being I. Wherever I go, *I* go, there is no leaving myself behind me. In moments of weakness or weariness we may wish to slough off our identity, we feel as Job did when he said to God—to God, mind you: "Thou wilt seek me, but *I shall not be*" (Job 7:21). But in hours of health, annihilation is not our hope or expectation—or so far as it is our expectation, we are horrified by it. I do exist. Non-being, as Tillich has been saying, is the great threat. The seeker for identity never feels satisfied short of some assurance of continuance, of permanence.[3]

Again, I am *I*. This also seems distressing to many. Wishing to be someone or something else is a common human trait. Walt Whitman felt that he could "turn and live with animals"; Robinson Jeffers has always gone "envying the quietness of stones."[4] Looking at it from a different angle, this is a very heartening discovery. I am I means that no one else is I. I *am* I—my existence is indefectible, unique. In the midst of all the fluctuating variables of life, I am I. In the midst of relationships pulling this way and that, in the midst of all the clamor and the invitations to become one of some kind of crowd, large or small, even in those intimate associations where one desires intensely to belong to, even to *be* a beloved Other, I am still I. However incomplete in myself, I am myself nevertheless. I am I, I am the kind of being who can say I and think I and be I. I am not *that*, as is claimed in the oriental religions. I am not a thing, for a thing is never I. I am not primarily a part of something else, I am first of all I. I am real, I am as real as anything else. I am so real that at times there comes a temptation to deny the reality of everything else and reign, a solipsist monarch, in a world of dreams. I am as real as God is real, though with a different grade or kind of reality. My reality is not something hard-wrung from an unwilling universe. My reality is something in the scheme of things; the universe would be the less if I were not I. God intends my reality, and upholds me in it; to destroy me you must first destroy God. I am I, though there may be (and there are) millions and billions of other egos, other selves, alike in our being yet infinitely varied in our capacities. I am I, the same who was I yesterday. I have learned something since then, I have forgotten something, the field of my awareness may be wholly changed from ten seconds ago; but I am still I, the same through my whole range of time. I am continuous, first, not with my qualities but with myself. Qualities and capacities change and grow and wither. Memory plays tricks and I seem—and am —many things to many men. But always the central self is *the* self, no other can take my place. Others may come to live where I live, as I live where others lived; the stream of life flows through us but we are not dissolved. I am I always. I may rejoice in this, or rail against it, but I accept it.

Yet the acceptance is a choice, and I am the one who must choose for me. I can do nothing, believe nothing, say nothing— in the last analysis learn nothing—without my own choice. I may feel assured of my freedom, I may feel conscious of unfreedom; but whether free or bound, my choice there must always be. Leading or following, the inner choice is always my own.

Bare identity is not the same thing as personality. Personality is a product of surrounding, of experience. To the personality of an individual, many other individuals contribute; but no contribution can be made to his identity. I cannot reach my destiny alone; but as it is I who must find the beginning of the road, it is still I who find or lose, am found or am lost, at the end of it. No other can knock for me at the first gate or answer for me at the last.

This identity of which I have been speaking is not lost by time nor by the changes which time brings. It is not broken by a gap in consciousness. It is not lost under however many layers of qualities. And *it is not lost by identification*. Without identification, identity fails of its end; but identity is not swallowed up by identification. To put it another way: identity is not nullified by the fact, if it be a fact, that only in identification can identity fully develop.

Christianity has a social interpretation and outworking which is valid and valuable, even indispensable. We shall be considering one aspect of it in some detail. Christian theology had a social theory of the self before the psychologists worked at it. But the Christian view of the self stands over against all purely and exclusively social theories, whether these are theological or not. I am always over-against, not opposed to but distinct from other men and God.[5]

The struggle or search for identity is not, therefore, properly a seeking for a missing or lost identity, for that is the one thing one has—because one IS—and cannot lose. The search, when successful, is a discovery of what was there always. It appears in many forms. In Miller's *Death of a Salesman,* the wife was seeking identity for her husband when she cried out, "Attention must be finally paid to such a person."[6] The husband of a "trapped housewife" in a TV series spoke to his wife about what happened to him every day. When I shave in the morning, mine is the only face in the mirror, he said. When I go in a car pool to the station I am one of five men. On the station platform I am one of sixty. In the city I am one of six million—a bit of dust, a nothing. When I come home at night I get my scattered pieces together. Home is the place where I can be myself. That is all true, in some degree, for all of us. But the man did not lose or break up his identity in the big city, he only came under the illusion of not having or not being one. The identity was always there.

The relation of identity to identification will be clearer when we have analyzed identification. But it should be said here that the relation is often obscured by terminology. The so-called quest for identity is actually, more often than not, a seeking for what we shall distinguish as identification. One wants to belong, is gregarious; one finds oneself, as it is said, in one's relationships.

Identity in the sense I mean is not synonymous with relationships; it is rather what is related. Something new is added through relationships; but the newness is not possible apart from the elemental I. Identity is that which itself cannot be exchanged, built up, shared. It is what no husband and wife achieve. Personalities can merge, but not identities. Harmony can be achieved, but there can no more be personal harmony without separate identity than there can be musical harmony without distinct and different tones. It is useless for seekers after identity to attempt to create it or have an expert create it for them; useless to try to work it up or to increase it. What can be sharpened, clarified, and intensified is the *awareness* of identity; and this will turn up as one of the types of identification.

Much of what has been said has an implicit theological background, but it would be true in any case. It is *only* from within a theological perspective, however, that one can answer the question, Why identity? How is it that I am I, that I *am* at all? The answer, however we may come by it, is that I am, by the will of God. Serious questions may distress me when I think, Why am I *as* I am? Why am I weak, timid, vacillating, overbearing, or what not—why do I have the qualities, especially the bad qualities, which I do have? I may blame myself for them, or my ancestors, or the devil, or God. But *that* I am, whatever be my qualities or deformities, is by the will of God. There is that in my life which a Reformed Christian would certainly say is contrary to God's will, in spite of the puzzles which such a proposition entails. But that I exist at all is not my own will, it is not the devil's intent; that is to say, my existence is not *per se* and *ipso facto* contrary to the pattern of the universe and destructive of it. I am not an accident, not something to be rubbed out, my existence does not, as such, produce a flaw in the clear crystal of ultimate Being. I am, because God wills it—because God wills *me*.

To appreciate this in the present context of identity and identification we have to be farther along than we are; so further discussion of this must be presently postponed.

Now, what is identification? Again I plead the privilege of making clear my intention in the use of a word which, to be sure, is not new, and has been used legitimately with various other intentions and connotations. To begin with, we do not call identification a doctrine. It belongs in the substructure of doctrine, it goes into the making of many doctrines. It can be used to test the validity of doctrine, but it is not a doctrine *per se*. It is never once mentioned in Scripture by name, nor has it been defined anywhere, so far as I know, as a doctrine, by any church. It is not required of a Christian doctrine, in Reformed circles, that it shall be mentioned in the King James Version by name, otherwise we should have no doctrine of the Trinity. But I am not proposing that identification should be promulgated as dogma. I am simply pointing out, *passim*, that the principle is latent in various actual dogmas and doctrines of the Christian church. Further, it is an observable phenomenon, and a matter of widely shared experience. It is one of those presuppositions of which we spoke at the beginning, and it is (I suggest) an indispensable, a vital one.

Let us attempt a definition, at first piecemeal, then putting it together in one sentence.

1. *Identification is a mental and moral act.* That is, it can take place silently; the identifier himself may even be unaware of its taking place in his mind. But still it is an act, as much so as any other mental act, such as decision, acceptance, rejection, and so on. It is also a moral act, or it can be moral. (It is not necessary to define "moral" since we all know what it means if no one asks us.) It may be hard to point to a mental act, or a physical one either, which in its context is not moral. But we might draw a distinction between moral and non-moral (not immoral or unmoral!) analogous to the distinction between personal and impersonal. If you think, "That's my banker," that is a non-moral proposition; making it has no moral connotations, probably, beyond the universal obligation to tell the truth. But if you say or think, "I hate that stingy, suspicious man," that is a moral act, taking (so to speak) a "stance" vis-à-vis the man in question.

Now identification, of the kind we mean, in all its forms is a moral as well as a mental act. There may be non-moral acts of identification; I think it can be shown that there are such, but these are not our concern.

2. *Identification involves understanding and will on the part of the one who makes the identification.* Identification may sometimes be automatic, unconscious, but some output of will there must be. Understanding is, of course, involved, since identification is capable of intelligible affirmation or denial open to rational discussion.

3. *Identification involves personal subjects.* Again, there may be identification on sub-personal or non-personal levels; but these, if they exist, are not the sort we are to deal with. The number of personal subjects is immaterial; but at least two are required for a true identification. As we shall see, the personal subjects involved are not necessarily *persons*.

4. *The personal subjects involved in an act of identification must be numerically different.* If I say that the president of the Colossus Corporation receives the highest salary paid anywhere in the world, and you reply, "I thought Mr. John Smith was the world's highest-paid executive," I might answer, "We are both right, for Mr. Smith is the president of Colossus." In popular usage, that would be identification, but that is not what I here mean by that word. That business about Mr. Smith simply calls attention to the fact that two verbal tags can be used interchangeably to refer to the same individual. There is no duality here, no separating and joining, there is only a clarification of the reference of certain words.

5. *The practical effect of an act of identification is that the two subjects are regarded and treated as in all possible respects the same.* Identification which does not issue in further attitudes and acts on the part of the identifier is not what we should have in mind. I say "in all possible respects the same" because it will be clear that there may be some impossible respects; but again these do not concern us.

Now, putting our definition together: *Identification is a*

*mental and moral act, involving understanding and will, relating
two or more personal subjects, numerically different, in such a
way that they are regarded and treated as in all possible respects
the same.*

Before examining the idea more closely, let us distinguish
some *types of identification.* Consider three entities, which for the
purpose of our discussion at this point will be three persons, A,
B, and C. Identification can occur in any one of five different
ways, which we may call types. In the first type, A identifies B
with C. In the second type, A identifies himself with B. In the
third type, A identifies B with himself. In the fourth, A, who had
supposed he was B, discovers he is A, and accepts this as a fact.
In the fifth—much like the fourth—A does not discover, but
knows that he is A, and either rejoices in the fact or regrets it.
(An attempt will be made to distinguish this type of identification from identity, but the point is not essential.)

It has already been pointed out that the relation of identity is
expressed in books of logic by the formula, A is A. That is, A is
not anything but A. A cannot be both A and non-A, though it
must be one of these, and therefore if A is A, A is not non-A. This
sounds silly, but it is important. The very word identity means
same-entity, and refers to one and the same entity, not two; but
identification refers to two entities at least. (One of these may
be imaginary, as will be seen later.) A common occurrence involving identity is the report that the identity of a hitherto
unknown criminal has been established, and that John Doe is he.
What we mean in such a connection is that John Doe and the
criminal, who we had hitherto supposed were two persons, are
one and the same person; they are in effect two designations, two
verbal tags as we said just now, for the same person. In establish-
ing identity, in this sense, we bring together two supposedly
different objects and demonstrate that they are one and the same
object, with different names or seen from different points of
view. In identity, the number of what you are referring to is
one, only one. Identification, on the other hand, has to do with
relations of objects (or, more properly, subjects) which remain
numerically plural, after the identification as well as before.

Let us now distinguish more fully these five types of identification. In Type 1 (as we may call it here for short), A identifies
B with C. In terms of our definition, A so relates B to C (in his
mind) that they are regarded and treated, by him, as in all possible respects the same. This type is external, yet not objective.
It is external because A simply makes the identification; he has
no part in it. It is external because it is not necessary that B or
C should know anything about it. They may, for example, be
generals, one in Carthage and one in the Confederate States of
America. The identifier (as in the famous cartoon) may point to
a portrait of Hannibal and say, "The Joseph B. Johnston of the
Punic Wars, sir!" This type is not necessarily objective, because
A may be quite mistaken in his judgment. An everyday example of this type is a situation where a man's relationships
with another man have been uniformly satisfactory, so that he
entertains toward the second man a steadily cordial attitude.
When introduced to the second man's brother, he identifies the
two, not confusing them so as to suppose they are identical,
but associating them mentally in such a way that his attitude to
the brother, even before he knows him at all well, is as cordial
as that toward the man he has known so long. This type of
identification includes the case where B is not an individual but
a group, and even A may be a group. A may be the general public; B may be a minority group; C may be someone who superficially resembles members of the group B, and is regarded and
treated by the general public as if he were a member of that
group. Witness the incidents involving African or Indian diplo-
mats in restaurants around Washington.

Type 2 may be called centrifugal and Type 3 centripetal.
Each may involve individuals or groups. In Type 2, A identifies himself with B; that is, he mentally and volitionally puts
himself outside himself and into another self. In an extreme case,
the subject may think he is Napoleon, or God; and is adjudged
insane. But there are perfectly normal forms of centrifugal
identification, such as a wife's identifying herself with her
husband, or a boy's identifying himself with his football team.

The subjects involved in this identification, as well as others, may not only be groups, but may be individuals who stand for groups, such as a college, church, or city. In Mississippi, it is said, in the courtroom the sheriff keeps his hat on at all times. This is not bad manners; it harks back to the old English courts, where, when the King's mace was brought in, all persons present were obliged to uncover—all but the sheriff. He was the King's personal representative, and so kept on his hat. He was identified with the Crown. No one supposed he *was* the Crown, but he was in that detail treated as if he were. The groups involved in identifications may be very large—racial or national. A Russian with a Russian name and a Russian appearance would have a hard time finding a job teaching school or teaching Sunday school in most places in America. He would, in most people's minds, be automatically identified with Communists, and Communists with atheists. Thus words like Southerner, Negro, Republican, and unnumbered others are praise-words or blame-words for individuals, as used by other individuals who identify persons properly bearing such names and yet perhaps improperly identified with whole groups (quite possibly imaginary groups) all members of which are thought to share the same supposedly pleasant or unpleasant characteristics. But to return to our types:

If Type 2 involves self-abnegation, Type 3 involves self-aggrandizement. In Type 3 the Self reaches out and seizes the Other and draws it into itself. Perhaps the most common form of Type 3 in everyday life is the possessive parent, who consciously or unconsciously regards the child as a sort of extension of his own personality. The aggressive businessman, the executive who must have his yes-men about him, likewise absorbs into his own energetic personality the selves of the men in the lower echelons. A further example of this is seen when an institution, a nation, or some lesser group becomes so absorptive and demanding that there is no room left for individual selfhood. All this may seem to imply that Type 3 is invariably bad, and indeed the extreme of badness is seen in demon-possession. C. S. Lewis, in his *Screwtape Letters*,[7] represents Satan and his minions as trying to absorb, to swallow up their victims, destroying their identity by merging it with their own. Readers of *Perelandra*[8] will recall Weston, the Un-man, whose personality was no longer his own but Satan's. Yet while this type of identification is usually bad, it is not bad when God is the agent, and may not be bad when men are the agents, as we shall have occasion to show.

Types 4 and 5 are mixed, and are presented with hesitation. They both involve identity, as the other types do not, and ordinarily occur only with individual subjects. In these types the second entity (B in our diagram) may not be a real one, but may exist only as a thought in the mind and imagination of the identifying agent.

Type 4 is a mental shift from one identity to another. It takes place in a situation in which an identity, hitherto latent in the subject's mind, or even actively rejected, is recognized and accepted. In terms of our diagram, A, who had been under the impression that he was B, discovers he *is* A and sadly or gladly accepts this as a fact. In the Bible, the classic example of this fourth type of identification is David after Nathan's accusation. David, who was a liar, an adulterer, and a murderer, not to say a hypocrite, did not think of himself in that light. He identified himself with an image in his mind, the image of the King who can do no wrong. When he heard the story that Nathan told, he was very far from saying, Well, the best of us are a long way from perfect; who are we to criticize this man you describe? On the contrary, David broke into a rage which (we may suppose) was quite genuine. Then came the moment of truth. Nathan said —quietly, I think; he didn't need to shout when he was speaking for the Holy Spirit—*You are the man.* And in a terrible flash David knew the prophet was right. He accepted the identification and made it his own. Thief, liar, all the rest of it—I am he, I am he. David does not identify himself with any culprit then in jail or liable to jail. He identifies himself with himself, a person whom up to that moment he had not even seen, the low scoundrel who would murder a loyal friend to steal the friend's wife.

Any man who accepts the truth, *I am a sinner*, furnishes an example of this fourth type of identification. The man and the sinner are numerically one; but in the man's mind, before he makes the identification, the sinning self is not the real self. We have all known the experience. If David had not accepted the truth, Nathan's "Thou art the man" would have had no effect. But when the identity was accepted and acknowledged, then it became identification; a moral event had occurred which was the beginning of transformation.

What I believe to be the outstanding example of Type 5 we shall observe in a later chapter. It may not be common. It is not so much a matter of identification as of identity, and even as identification it is more a matter of attitude than of will. Properly speaking, it is an attitude toward a long recognized identity. Logically speaking, it could be omitted from the list of types, but psychologically it belongs here. A simple illustration of what is meant comes from the experience of a little boy who for most of the first ten years of his life always wanted to be older than he was. At the age of ten he was still wanting to be twelve or any decent age . . . till he read in the *Youth's Companion* a story about a ten-year-old boy. It dawned on him that even a ten-year-old could be important enough to have a story printed about him. From that time on throughout his life, boy and man, he happily identified himself with his age, whatever it was. Now that child knew for months: I am a ten-year-old. But he didn't like it. Then came the change. It was not a change in the calendar nor in his relation to the calendar. It was a change in how he felt about his relation to the calendar. This can work in reverse, of course, and a man who has always known himself to be a poor man, but has never lost any sleep over it, realizes one day with a shock that he really is poor. It is not, however, the element of discovery or of sudden change that distinguishes Type 5—that is the characteristic feature of Type 4. The characteristic of Type 5 is the intense emotional attitude toward what one knows oneself to be, a willing of the inevitable, a rejoicing in what cannot be otherwise, an enthusiastic identification with identity.

Types 4 and 5 both bring out the point that identification

is dynamic; identity is static—not dead, *static*. Identification goes beyond identity. Identity is *so*, apart from any judge, and without any agent. Identification can take place only as an act of will and choice. Identity is objective in the sense that no act of recognition, will, or personal choice is required for it to be true. Identification is always subjective, always personal, since an act of will is called for. Identity in itself is not moral, not immoral either. It is a simple datum. Identification is always moral. I mean it has a moral quality or dimension, though it may conceivably be, and sometimes is, immoral. Identity cannot be created, not now. When and as God creates individuals he creates each one identical with itself; but no act on a creature's part can either create identity where it was not, or destroy it where it is. Identity cannot be altered. If A is A it can never be non-A. If the A that is A changes, so must the A that A is. Each changes when and as the other does, because there are not two A's, there is only one A. In identification, on the other hand, one of the two members can change so that identification becomes no longer possible. Identification therefore depends on a sustained exertion of will united to the understanding and usually to the imagination too, rather than on one single act of will. The same identification may at times be asserted, at times repudiated.[9]

Now, let us inquire about the reality, the validity, and the justification of identification. For purposes of this discussion I should like to distinguish among the terms "real," "valid," and "justified." Let me first illustrate from a business contract. If I find among the papers of a man a note saying "Call G. B. Jones," that is not a contract, not a real contract, only a memorandum. However, if this man has an agreement with someone drawn up so that it is legally binding, then it is a contract, both real and valid. If the contract is fully drawn up but lacks some small feature, let us say the notary's seal in a state where that is required, then it is a real contract but not a valid one. The lawyer will say, "This contract is invalid"; he will not say, "This love letter," or "This request for a raise," is not valid. One speaks of the invalidity of a contract which despite its invalidity is nevertheless a contract, not a note to the milkman. And yet a valid contract, from a business standpoint, might represent an unwise policy and so be unjustified.

I know that *real* and *valid* are words often used interchangeably, but I need to make some distinction. To take another example, there may be in your basement or attic a couple of contraptions. One of these is a phonograph, one is a baby carriage. Now the baby carriage is not a phonograph at all, it is not a real phonograph. The phonograph, however, while it is real enough, is not valid, because it will not function. It has lost its needle and can't be played. But suppose you owned a phonograph which was both real and valid, but all you did with it was to play rock-and-roll from dusk to midnight every night? Then as your neighbor I would say that the phonograph, although real and valid, was not justified.

With regard to identification, some types at any rate may be real without being valid. An identification is real when anyone makes it. It is valid only if the identification, when made, corresponds to the facts as they are. Identification, in other words, is valid when it rests on truth, invalid when it rests on untruth. We may put this in another way by going back to participation. Unless the identifier, the agent of identification, feels that the two subjects identified (of which he may be one) share some things in common, he will at least hesitate to make the identification. You may use the terms interpenetrate, overlap, share, participate, interflow, interfuse, or the word used, for example, by George L. Prestige and Charles Williams—coinhere.[10] Using the word "participation," we must say: No participation, no identification. "Black is white"; no participation, therefore untrue, therefore not valid. "Khrushchev is a Communist"; he does participate in Communism, therefore a valid identification. "John A. Mackay is a Communist"; he does not participate in Communism, therefore untrue, therefore not a valid identification. Incidentally, using the terminology I am temporarily adopting, even a false accusation, a slander, may be a "real" identification, of Type 1, however false it may be. You say I am in the narcotics racket; a real identification, but a false one and invalid. No amount of accusation, when it is false, can establish an identification as valid if there is no actual participation.[11]

This raises the question of participation itself. Participation does not, in itself, produce or induce identification. Participation may proceed for a long time without anyone's noticing it; or it may be noticed but nothing made of it. Nevertheless, without participation, actual or alleged, there is no identification. The problem here is: What exactly *is* participation, and how great an extent or degree of it is required for identification? If the great Plato never made quite clear what he meant by participation, no more can I. As a working notion, we may say that in the present context, whenever some vital, i.e., essential, points, areas, aspects, or features of the entities in question are felt to be similar or even the same, this likeness or sharing of quality or qualities is what is meant by participation. The similarity, of course, must be a vital one. Two left-handed men have their left-handedness in common; but very few people would allege an identification on this ground alone. On the other hand, a sex criminal and the hijacker of a plane, very different human types, have in common an antisocial attitude that is felt to be vital, and enough to establish an identity so far as the penal code is concerned. To be sure, identifications are made by some people on ludicrously inadequate grounds. What may be called the threshold of identification differs in different persons. But whenever the identifier is convinced that the similarities or identities of essence or qualities are so strong as to warrant classifying both objects together and treating them identically, there participation has reached, for that agent, the identification point. We shall run into some very notable exceptions to this.

Now to review those types again, with an eye to validity and justification. Take the case where A (let us call him Alexander) has been cheated by Benjamin Doe. Later he meets Charles Doe, Benjamin's brother, and without further inquiry so identifies Charles with Benjamin that he regards Charles also as a liar and a cheat. For Alexander, the fact that these men are physically brothers is enough participation to warrant identification. If Charles is an honest man, however, then the two brothers do not share in the very quality most to the point in the case. The identification is invalid entirely. Yet *in A's mind* there is a real identification, and this works out in behavior; Alexander treats the good Charles with the same contempt he shows toward the black sheep Benjamin. Alexander is believing something false; yet his *belief* is real, all too real perhaps. This of course does not make it valid. The belief is a genuine belief, it may have extensive consequences; psychologically and sociologically it is no different from other beliefs he may entertain which are *not* contrary to fact, as this one is. Furthermore, Alexander may be sincere and consistent in his conviction. But the identification is invalid all the same. An invalid identification, especially of Type 1, is a verbal thing, no more. I can say, Black is white; F. D. Roosevelt was the grandson of Theodore Roosevelt; all Russians are supermen. If I am crazy enough I can suppose anything. But thoughts that are real are not necessarily true.

In Types 2 and 3 validity, or truth, and reality blend. In these cases the identifier, instead of making a judgment about two other persons, thrusts himself into the identification. The possessive mother who cherishes the child simply for the enlargement of her own aggressive ego (Type 3) may not clearly verbalize the identification she is making; but by her attitude she makes the identification not only real but valid. On the other hand, the mother who worships her child, and devotes herself to it even to the great detriment of her own proper interests; or the servant of his country who wears himself out in the service of the country with which he has long identified himself—these also (Type 2) in the very act of identification make it not only real but valid. It is only in Type 1 that an identification can be real without being valid.

Now, a valid identification may still not be justified. Of an invalid identification, all talk of justification is pointless. But a real and valid identification may be justified or not justified.

There are two criteria of justification, one particular, one general. (The fact that they are not easily established should make us cautious about making some identifications.) (1) In particular: *What does this identification do to personality?* At some point or other we must accept some basic value. For us (following Jesus, as we believe), that basic value is the personal human self. Whenever this value is hampered, minimized, debased, or destroyed, then the identification which produced such a result is unjustified. (2) The other criterion, very general, is: *What effect does the identification have upon the sum of good in the world?* If a man identifies himself with a socially harmful movement (an example of Type 2), as for example one with the purpose of impeaching an unimpeachable (though, being human, not impeccable) Chief Justice, the identification is a bad one, not because such an identification is invalid, but because it enhances the evil in this world. Similarly, a gang of thieves taking into their membership an innocent child would be a genuine act of identification, Type 3, but a bad, unjustified action, all the worse if fully successful.

Many interesting questions may be asked about these matters, but we have to forego them. As an example, is it possible to redeem an unjustified identification by substituting another which will be the exact opposite? As a specific case, take our possessive parent again. If it is a mistake to dissolve another's personality in one's own (Type 3), can such a parent set things right by making the opposite identification, Type 2, and dissolve his or her own personality in that of the child? Such a question can have no general answer. Each case must be examined on its own merits with regard to those two questions, What does the identification do to human personality, and to the sum of human good?

There is a striking case in the New Testament which illustrates several of these points at once. When Satan invited Jesus to fall down and worship him, he was inviting Jesus to identify himself with supreme evil, for worship is the ultimate example of identification, Type 2. Let us first assume that Jesus could have assented, and then assume that he could not have assented, and see where we come out. Let us assume that Jesus could have assented, and did assent, and so identified himself with Satan in the terms worshiper—worshiped. Even if, to your mind, Satan is one of those things that need to be demythologized, the point is that in yielding to this temptation the whole being and effort of Jesus would be allied in the most intimate way with all that stands up against God. In all real worship, the worshiper's consent is given, he does truly identify his purposes with those of the object of his worship. Now if Jesus had merged his purposes with the devil's, the action would have been real if Jesus had entered into it, and it would have been valid in our special sense of the word, because the purpose of Jesus, in that case, would have been, actually, the same as Satan's. Yet it would have been unjustified, because the discreative power of evil would have been by so much enhanced; unjustified because in that case Jesus' personality would have been shattered to the core, and nothing would have been left but a devil's pawn, a personality eaten out and destroyed.

On the other hand, if you take the view that Christ could *not* have succumbed to temptation, could not have assented to the devil's desire, that his nature and his person were such that worshiping Satan was not only unthinkable but inherently impossible, then you are affirming not simply that the proposed identification would have been unjustified, but that it would have been invalid and unreal. The suggestion would have been merely verbal; nothing would have happened. If Christ by an act of will *could* have radically altered his basic purpose, then such an identification, if made, would have been valid, no matter how vastly wrong it would have been. But if he himself was incapable of such an act as willingly worshiping evil, then the identification could not even have been real, to say nothing of being valid. Indeed, this case supports the statement that only in Type 1 can you have a real identification that is not valid. In Type 1 the identifier has no part in the identification except to think it true. The members of the identification, if we may call them so, can be joined in the identifier's mind without the slightest inclination toward each other in fact. But in all other types, as with this temptation of Jesus, the identifier is personally involved, and there is no way for the identification to be real without being valid as well. All this will become clearer when we examine specific doctrines which embody and illustrate, in one way or another, these types of identification, both invalid and valid.

3. I Some Unjustified *Identifications*

It has been said that the principle of identification can be used as a test of Christian doctrine. If a doctrine does not involve this principle, then of course it cannot be used as a test. The doctrine, for example, of God's spirituality or of his infinity does not, so far as I can now see, make use of our principle. So it is with such doctrines as that of the so-called Intermediate State, or of the alleged impeccability of angels.

However, if all the doctrines in which this principle is presupposed or explicitly propounded were removed from our theological structures, or if the support which the principle gives them were removed, the gaps would be many, and would be fatal to a systematic, not to say Christian, theology. Yet not all doctrines making some use of or resting wholly or in part on the principle of identification are soundly based. Not that the principle is faulty or fanciful; rather the trouble—when there is trouble—is that the framers of the doctrine in question, whether consciously or not, have used the principle in unjustified ways.

To review our conclusions to this point for a moment: An identification may be unjustified for any one of three reasons. It may be unjustified because invalid. This should go without saying, for invalid (in our context) means not founded on fact, not true. Again, an identification, even if valid, may be unjustified if it does harm to human personality—or, I might add, if it slanders the divine character—or plainly lessens the sum of human good.

An objection could be raised at this point. Is not this the old hedonistic calculus again, and is there any way of measuring the sum total of human good, or even the net good experienced by one man? I would reply that, for one thing, "good" and "pleasant" are not at all synonymous, but that on the other hand, those high passages in the New Testament which exalt love as the heart of God's law and will for man, involve some sort of calculus. Unless we take thought to enhance love, we shall too often be acting in ways that destroy love. Yet the good life is not a calculating sort of life, a balancing of tiny weights of good and evil. That way lies Pharisaism. Moral maturity, for the Christian not less than for anyone else, comes as a skill, an art, which has at first to be learned—the art of living in line with the calculus without often stopping, as the Pharisees did, to make calculations. The Christian develops a kind of immediate perception—call it intuition, a sensitiveness to the Holy Spirit, or what you will—as to what is good in the sense of productive-of-good. The truly good person, the artist in the good life, like all artists becomes more and more able to do with ease and grace and without hesitation what once he had to work out from difficult rules. The artist, it has been said, swallows all rules. So I would not say that everyone can always be sure about this sum of human good. But there are choices where it is plain, except to those confused by stupidity or blinded by malice, in which direction the largest good is to be found.

We shall take a look now at four doctrines or dogmas which as I see them are shaky or untenable, on account of undergirding identifications which are for one reason or another unjustified. They may be shaky for other reasons, but we are considering only one, the kind of identification involved. The first three of these are forms of false or invalid identifications of the human and the divine. The fourth is a different type of identification but equally unjustified. Universal agreement here is not to be expected. Who can expect universal agreement throughout Christendom if he comes down on one side of any fence? Concerning one of these doctrines almost all orthodox Christians, certainly in the

West, would agree. About the second, all Reformed theology would agree. As to the third, there is a mixed multitude on each side; while on the fourth, opinion among Reformed thinkers will vary. Some would say we are beating a dead horse; others would accuse us of attacking a central Christian truth.

1. First is the doctrine, in its various forms, of *divinized humanity:* that is to say, a belief that now or later a human being is or is to be so taken into the divine nature that he is absorbed into the infinite Unity which is God. Now in authentic Christianity, some identification of God and man is a vital principle. But in the doctrine now in question, it is not identification that is affirmed but identity in whole or in part.

(a) Consider a low form of this: the Mormon doctrine that God has a body like men.[1] This is not mysticism. Indeed it puts mysticism out of the question. A God with a physical body can no more be united to other physical beings than we can be joined physically with one another. This particular notion is the reverse of mysticism, for it assimilates God to man, rather than the other way around. It localizes God, it makes him an empirical being among others, a part of the material universe.

This idea is so foreign to the whole line of Christian thought from the beginning that it hardly calls for mention at all. But it is obvious that any notion which un-deifies God is plainly wrong. To be sure, this particular doctrine as believed in America is not consciously based on an identification, but rather on literal interpretations of anthropomorphisms in the Bible. Using the same method, one could comb the Old Testament and come out with a God who would be sub-human, altogether sub-personal. But to return to the construction of the Latter-Day Saints, the great majority of Christians would agree that there is an invalid identification here. What is said about God, especially in the Old Testament, is interpreted as meaning exactly what it would mean if said of man. The body of God is identical with the body of any man, in the same sense that all men's bodies are identical in qualities. If God differs from man it is as Goliath differs from David. Also, this view has the more serious result of turning the Trinity into a tri-theism, liable to all the criticisms which can be fairly made of such a notion.

Another way to look at this is to observe that the identification of God's body, or the references to it, with physical bodies such as we all experience, is unscriptural; therefore false and so invalid. Mormons with whom I have talked argue that their position is scriptural, by which of course they mean in accordance with a literal interpretation of certain passages, ignoring others that conflict. The question of when to take Scripture literally is not our problem; but it must be said here that when any theological construction affirms or implies what is in outright contradiction to the major overall representations or spirit of Scripture, that construction is more than suspect. And it is the consensus of Christendom, and has always been so, that God is spirit, not body.[2]

(b) Another form of this identification of God and man is seen in various types of pantheism, but also in one variety of orthodox faith. In the Eastern Orthodox Church there is the assertion and promise of sharing the divine nature, not as present fact but as future hope.[3] Salvation is indeed sometimes defined as the transformation of our very being from finite to infinite, from human to divine. The western church has nearly always held it to be axiomatic that "*finitum non capax infiniti*," the finite cannot contain the infinite, cannot be or become infinite. The Roman Catholic Church, with all the special veneration shown to Mary, insists on Mary's creaturehood. Catholic and Protestant are alike on this point: the line between Creator and creature is not to be crossed by any creature, not the highest and most God-like.[4]

In the western church it is said that the Eastern Orthodox construction runs counter to the New Testament. The Orthodox proof-text their doctrine with Second Peter 1:4; western churches either explain away Second Peter or point out that the apostolic authenticity and canonicity of Second Peter is open to question, and therefore this epistle is not to be taken as a quarry for proof-texts of any basic doctrine; or else point out that whatever be thought of the canonicity of the epistle, if we take the Bible as a whole the indefectible and eternal transcendence of God is made so unmistakably plain (by plain is not meant simple), that we have no right to promulgate as dogma anything contrary to it. In short, we would say that the alleged identification, amounting to identity, of human nature with divine nature (whatever meaning "nature" may have) is false, because of the overwhelming testimony of Scripture at all levels, and false because metaphysically impossible if we accept the apparent truism, *Finitum non capax infiniti*.[5]

(c) More widely held forms in which this kind of identification has been worked out are seen in the many varieties of mysticism in the western as well as in the eastern church. (I personally dislike to criticize mystics and mysticism. For one thing, some mystics are wonderful characters; for another, I may seem to be casting aspersions on more justifiable types of mysticism, or denying any element of it in true Christian faith. This is not my intention.) The Eastern Orthodox doctrine, if I understand it, is not that we do now partake of the divine nature, but that we shall, if we work at it. But the more general sort of mysticism affirms that we are now one, ontologically one, with God, and that what we need is not to achieve this so much as to realize it, namely, that God's essence is our essence, his being our being.[6] Mysticism has always hovered on the edge of main-line Christianity, but has for the most part been repudiated. This is not the so-called Christ-mysticism, but that more diffused kind which ignores the doctrine of the Trinity or knows only the Holy Spirit. Reformed theology has been especially antipathetic to mysticism, for obvious reasons.

One ground on which mysticism is more than open to suspicion is the dubious validity of its underlying identification, which amounts to a declaration and discovery of identity. Some *identification* with God, as Christians are aware, lies at the heart of Christian theology and life. But *identity with God* is another matter. No one who takes the Biblical revelation seriously can dare to assert this identity. Of course, the mystic does not claim to be the whole of God, but he does claim to melt into Deity (as it were) so that there is no dividing line—the I-Thou vanishes and there is only the ineffable One.[7] Applying our criteria of justification, we have to say that mysticism, whether of the Buddhist, Hindu, or Christian type, involves an identification which is unjustified on three different grounds. The identification is real in the sense that it is made, it is affirmed and believed. But it cannot make good its claim to truth; it cheapens personality, and it tends to decrease the sum of human good. A brief look at each of these points:

Mysticism cannot make good its claim to truth. (It cannot be disproven either, it should be admitted.) Granted the underlying metaphysic of monism, and granted the validity of subjective experiences, or rather subjective interpretation of subjective experiences, there is simply no way to disabuse the mystic of his convictions. His ultimate truth lies, or flies, beyond logic, hence cannot be attacked by logic. But in the light of all the arguments for pluralism it is saying too much to affirm that monism is the only possible metaphysic. And in the light of the ethical results, or lack of results, and the darkness of the theological analysis (see below), the mystic, if he has made his case, has made it to himself but hardly to the world.

As for the effect of mysticism on personality, a characteristic of such mystical writers as I have read is that personality, in the sense of individuation and individuality, is rated low if not denied. In the height of the mystical rapture the sense of personal identity of which we have spoken is lost; I am no longer I, I am blessedly lost in the Infinite One. One with the One . . . Thou art That. Not, Thou art inseparable from That; nor Thou art the child of That—Thou *art* That. Dr. Roland M. Frye, of Emory University, has shown neatly the contrast between Hinduism of the Vedanta type and Christian thought. To the Hindu mind, the trouble with man is ignorance, not sin; the basic ignorance is not knowing that one is God; and salvation is the knowledge that God and man are one—not at one, but one. To the Christian mind, the trouble with man is not ignorance but sin; and the basic sin is supposing that one *is* God; salvation involves getting rid of the illusion, which for the Hindu is salvation itself. At the risk of sounding ill-natured, I am not going to resist the temptation to remind you what kind of God it is with whom or with which the mystic supposes himself to be one. This is from the conclusion of the *Mystical Theology* of "Dionysius the Areopagite." He says:

> We maintain that It is not soul, or mind, or endowed with the faculty of imagination, conjecture, reason, or understanding; nor is It any act of reason or understanding; nor can It be described by the reason or perceived by the understanding, since It is not number, or order, or greatness, or littleness . . . and since It is not immovable nor in motion, or at rest, and has no power, and is not power or light, and does not live, and is not life; nor is It personal essence, or eternity, or time; nor can It be grasped by the understanding, since It is not knowledge or truth . . . nor is It one, nor is It unity, nor is It Godhead or Goodness; nor is It a Spirit, as we understand the term, since It is not Sonship or Fatherhood . . . nor does It belong to the category of non-existence or to that of existence; nor do existent beings know It as it actually is, nor does It know them as they actually are; nor can the reason attain to It to name It or to know It; nor is It darkness, nor is It light, or error, or truth; nor can any affirmation or negation apply to It; . . . we apply not unto It either affirmation or negation, inasmuch as It transcends all affirmation by being the perfect and unique Cause of all things, and transcends all negation by the pre-eminence of Its simple and absolute nature—free from every limitation and beyond them all.[8]

You can see what identity with *That* would do for personality. When any mystic tells me, Thou art That, I can only reply, I do hope not! and I welcome a Christian messenger who will assure me, Thou are not That; sinner thou art, but not utter nonsense, *thohu-wavohu,* without form and void! I admit to a prejudice: I feel a greater affinity with that blunt writer St. James, who wrote: "The wisdom from above is . . . open to reason" (James 3:17).

(3) As for the effect on the sum of human good, unquestionably every mystical rapture adds to the sum of human happiness;

but viewed in the light of contributions to human *good,* while one does not wish to press comparisons, one may suggest a look at parts of the world where pantheism of this sort has held undisputed sway for centuries, and see what are the ethical results. Our American brand of pantheism (which repudiates the name) nevertheless asserts clearly: There are no souls, there are no spirits, there is only one spirit, and that is God's. So far as we are souls we are God's soul.[9] Not to repeat all the reasons for doubting the validity of this alleged identity, all main-line Christianity has been distinctly suspicious of a world-view in which, logically and actually, there is no room for evil. The most effective way to assure the continuance of a disease is to deny its existence.

2. Most of the Christian church would agree with what has been said thus far. The majority of western Christians, i.e., the Roman Catholic Church, will not see the fairness in the next illustration of unjustified identification, but Protestants see it without difficulty. It is the identification of Mary the mother of Jesus with the Queen of Heaven. Here we have a curious case, of the identification of an actual historical person with a very widely believed-in character straight out of Middle East mythology. The Hebrew religion, we are told, was the only one in the welter of religions around the Fertile Crescent that did not have a Queen of Heaven. Popularly, of course, one was demanded. Readers of Jeremiah will recall that prophet's difficulties with the women who insisted on worshiping that Queen; and followers of archaeology will think of the temple at Elephantine where JHWH and a consort were conjointly worshiped.[10]

There are psychological reasons for all this, but such reasons are not in themselves an excuse. Identification of a real person with an imaginary person is invalid and unjustified on the face of it. Aside from this, there is no hint in the New Testament that (as a Catholic might claim) the position of Queen of Heaven was never an actual one till it was created for Mary. Again the Protestant verdict is negative. As we observe Mariolatry, more properly mario-hyperduliatry if there were such a word, from

the outside, as we see it around the world, we find it, so far from
contributing to the sum of good, actually no different, in its
effects, from acknowledged idolatries. Once in a summer school
course in religion I had made some remarks about the virtual
polytheism of the Roman church, and a young man, a good
Catholic, took time afterward to remonstrate with me. "Would
you not be glad to know your mother is praying for you?" he
asked. "Yes, of course." "And would it make any difference that
she is praying in heaven?" "Not at all," I said. "Then what is
wrong if I pray to Mary and she prays to Christ and he prays to
God?" "Well," I said, "why not pray to God direct?" "I never
thought of that," he said. That is precisely the harm that alleged
Queens of Heaven do: they distract attention and devotion from
the one true God. It was no violent anti-Catholic, it was a professor at the Yale Graduate School, who pointed out that Christianity, in most of its history, has been polytheistic.[11] He was
thinking of this very business of praying to these official executive assistants to Deity. Incidentally, the professor was approv-
ing of it, for the reason that like "Dionysius" he did not see how
the High God could be an object of prayer.

3. Protestants are divided on the next example to which I
refer. A minority of them agree with the Roman church, but at
any rate the Reformed family does not, that the church is the
"extension of the Incarnation." Augustine lent his support to the
idea, and a contemporary theologian so little tied to creedalism
as Dr. Nels F. S. Ferré has quoted Augustine with approval[12]
that Christ *and the church* are the complete Christ. Bishop
Lesslie Newbigin's commentary on the idea is the most succinct
and convincing criticism of this idea known to me.[13] Only a few
comments are necessary here. First, it would be quite wrong to
deny *any* kind or degree of identification between Christ and the
church. All Christian writers insist on a very intimate and indis-
soluble association indeed. But this theory of the extension of
the Incarnation goes beyond identification to assert identity; and
this is going farther than the truth warrants. In the Apostolic
age, when if ever one would expect to find someone affirming

of the church that it carried on the Incarnation, we do not hear this. The church is called the Body and Christ the Head, the church is said to have its being "in Christ"—an important thought for our thesis; the church is said to be the family of Christ, or his bride, or the building in which he is the chief cornerstone, or the garden which belongs to him. The church is the continuator of his work and the bearer of his Spirit; but it is not himself. Christ became man, not a church-man.

It is quite right to think of the church as a vital result of the Incarnation, as carrying on the work and teachings of Christ. But it is wrong—that is to say, invalid and untrue—to identify Christ with the church as an extension of his Incarnation. There is not even a full analogy between Jesus Christ, in the days of his flesh or now, and the actual empirical living church. If for no other reason, the analogy limps because in the actual Jesus Christ, the human person was one and undivided, whereas in the church there are many men of many minds. There was nothing un-Christlike about Christ, but there is much that is un-Christlike about the church. If we are going to think of it as an extension of the Incarnation, we may as well admit that it is inferior to the original. The suggestion that the church extends the Incarnation is false to fact if the qualities of the church and Christ are confused or identified, and is still more off-center if the functions of Christ and the church are identified. As Dr. Newbigin says, the church is a body of forgiven sinners, most imperfectly saved as yet; this was not true of Jesus. It was said of Christ that he who knew no sin was made to be sin for us; but this must not be said of the church, which does know sin and which can in no sense be made to be sin on anyone's behalf. The idea is therefore misleading and in some ways downright untrue. I venture to say that it can be a harmful idea too; for if taken seriously it leads to the delusion that the church can do no wrong.

4. Now we come to a doctrine or dogma which is found in the Reformed tradition but nowhere else; a doctrine which while professedly Biblical is only dubiously so, and seen in the light of

the principle of identification has many thin spots, not to say holes. I refer to the doctrine of the imputation of Adam's first sin, as presented in the Westminster Standards (Confession of Faith, Chapter VI, §III) and developed at length in the "Protestant Scholastics."[14] The word *imputation* suggests identification, for it suggests etymologically thinking-into, or thinking-in, which is the first feature of identification as we are using the term. It also suggests the problem of make-believe, something the mind does not merely accept or recognize but rather in some sense creates.

The problem is: How is the sin of Adam, specifically his first sin, connected with every individual since that time? There are many problems here which can be disregarded. We can, for instance, waive one question which to some has seemed important: Is the story of Genesis 3 to be taken literally? The dogma as we have it in our Confession of Faith was formed under the conviction, no doubt, of the "literal factual actuality" of those early chapters of the Bible; but the problem is not materially altered by denying that kind of factuality and placing the story in the realm of parable or myth. A recent scholarly defense of the dogma, John Murray's *Imputation of Adam's Sin*,[15] at the outset rejects the understanding of the story as a myth, in opposition to C. H. Dodd and Emil Brunner.[16] Dr. Murray deals throughout with the Adam story as with literal historical fact, somewhat stylized for theological use. But this hardly seems essential. Undoubtedly there was a first man somewhere, sometime, however he came to be. And in all likelihood the first man committed the first sin. Or if that seems too much, let us agree at least that there was a first sin of a first sinner, a first human sinner. I am aware of Kierkegaard's idea that sin presupposes sinfulness; but this seems to me to start an infinite regress, and is beside our point here, which has to do with conscious sin. Surely there was a first one! The problem still remains: What is the connection between that sin and my sin, between that sin and me? The doctrine of imputation is one of the church's attempts to explain how it is that God regards me as a sinner. As the doctrine of sin is presented in our Confession and Catechisms, two explanations are offered, and they are quite different though not necessarily in conflict. For the present we separate out not the doctrine of imputation in general, but the imputation of Adam's sin.

That God regards all men as sinners, all Christians agree. That all men *are* sinners, is also agreed. (How can we deny it?) Now, as God looks at us and at all men, does Adam's sin come into the picture each time? Readers of A. H. Strong's *Systematic Theology*[17] will recall his schematic representation of the various theories of imputation. I shall disregard the first three of these and the fifth (called by him Pelagian, Arminian, New School, and Placean), as they do not raise our problem; and look only at the fourth, the federal theory, one of the two which are combined in our Standards. On the federal theory, which Dr. Strong did not hold, nor did the redoubtable Dr. Shedd, but which was still taught in a strict form at Princeton in my student days, the sin of Adam, or rather the guilt of it,[18] is imputed directly, immediately, to every human being, apart from and logically prior to his inherited nature, and apart from any sin committed voluntarily or involuntarily by the man himself. As one of my professors at Princeton explained it to me personally, each man is damned (his word) three ways: (1) He is damned on account of the imputed guilt of Adam. (Whether the sin or the guilt be imputed makes no difference with the point; guilt alone without the sin would be enough to carry the curse of God.) Even if a man did not inherit an evil disposition, which he does, and even if he lived a perfect life, which he does not, he would be born a lost soul. Dr. A. A. Hodge tries to lighten the curse a little by saying that the antenatal condemnation does not involve the positive curse which is the penalty for willful sin; it is only the complete withdrawal of the Holy Spirit and the influences of the Spirit which are necessary for salvation. God, on this view, does not exactly kill the soul beforehand; he only withdraws or withholds the possibility and the means of life. (2) Each person is damned on account of (i.e., as a penalty for) the sinful nature which he inherits. (3) He is damned on account of his own sins, for the first act which any and every human being does, is invariably and inevitably a sinful act.

It is far from true that the federal theology is the standard theory of the church; it is a peculiarity of the Dutch and Scottish creeds. As is well known, this construction had been worked out by Cocceius, though not first by him, shortly before the Westminster Standards were adopted, and so was new at that time, in that form. The basic idea in it is that there was a covenant or contract, made between God and Adam, by the terms of which Adam's obedience or disobedience, with regard to one particular command of God, was to be credited or imputed—set to the account, as merit or guilt, for good or ill—to each of Adam's descendants severally and individually.[19] Dr. A. A. Hodge said, "It is obvious . . . that . . . the immediate imputation of the guilt of Adam's sin is to the race as a whole, and respects each individual antecedently to his existence as a judicial cause of his commencing that existence in a depraved condition."[20] Charles Hodge put the whole idea very simply: "Men . . . stood their probation in Adam. . . . evils which they suffer are . . . judicial inflictions. The loss of original righteousness, and death spiritual and temporal under which they commence their existence, are the penalty of Adam's first sin."[21]

This doctrine, in this form, has fallen by the wayside. The federal-theology explanation is not mentioned in the Presbyterian (U.S.) *Brief Statement of Belief* (1962), and it is also absent from the Presbyterian (U.P.U.S.A.) *Brief Statement of the Reformed Faith* (see Article 5). The creed of the United Church of Canada, which is Calvinist at base, and the Draft Catechism of the Church of Scotland have still less to say of this, if one may speak of less than nothing. In all my life I have yet to hear a sermon on Imputation as the federal theology sets it forth. Dr. L. Berkhof pointed out that the doctrine flourishes nowadays chiefly in churches of Dutch origin.[22] It also is a cardinal point in at least one denomination which regards the main-line Presbyterian churches as heretical or apostate.

Now there must be some reason for the desuetude of a dogma in a church which still officially supports it. One reason, of course, is the increased emphasis on the authority of Scripture as the source of doctrine; for there is no actual scriptural ground for the theory of the Adamic Covenant in the contractual form which is assumed in the federal theology, and hence none for this particular theory of imputation.[23] All the efforts to exhibit the doctrine in Scripture—and there have been some ingenious ones—break down over the simple fact that it is not there. If I were approaching the problem exegetically I think I could demonstrate this; but all I am trying to do is to apply the principle of identification, so we must get on. Our creed does contain some extra-Biblical ideas, so that it would seem that the mere fact that a doctrine cannot be proved from direct Scripture texts is not the sole motive for leaving a doctrine forgotten and untaught. There must be some other motive for the neglect of this once honored doctrine. I suggest that it is felt—though perhaps not explicitly—that it violates the principle of identification.

The identification involved here is Type 1. God views each man as Adam; or, conversely, views Adam as each man.[24] No man *is* Adam except Adam himself. Both Creationist and Traducianist draw a numerical distinction between each man and all other men, including Adam. Indeed, some of the most vigorous proponents of the federal theory have been Creationists by preference, e.g., L. Berkhof. On this theory, then, no man is Adam, no man has committed Adam's sin. But—*God treats each person as if he had committed Adam's sin.* Here is a clear case of two separate persons, one a person who has not committed a certain act, the other a person who has committed that act, yet both regarded and treated in the same way. The curse of God, without being withdrawn from the one, is extended to the other. The guilt of one, the penalty of one, is transferred to the other, and God proceeds to regard this other—meaning every person in the world to the end of time—just as if he had incurred the guilt and were liable to the penalty. In our little diagram, A is God, B is Adam, C stands for any other person. The curse of God is extended to C without regard for what he is, has done, or will do. It should be remembered that this "antenatal" condemnation is not sentence passed in advance for what the man is sure to do if he lives. It is a penalty for what his official representative did. What the one does, is set to the account of the other.[25]

Now, we have to bear in mind that this alleged act of identification on God's part may not be real. It is a real identification, to be sure, demonstrably so on the part of theologians; less demonstrable, and I suggest not demonstrable at all, on the part of God. But suppose, for argument's sake, that it be real, is it valid and is it justified?

If our analysis is correct, then as just said, this is an identification of Type 1. It is external; but it is subjective. On our tentative hypothesis, it is a real identification—i.e., A (God) has, in fact, same attitude toward B (Adam) and C (all other human beings). Even if B and C know nothing of this, and even if there were no connection whatever between B and C, A may still persist in this identification. There is no stopping a prejudice. So it can be said, and it has been said by proponents of this theory, that since God is sovereign, he can do as he will, and will as he will. In terms of our make-believe, this would be the equivalent of saying that since God is sovereign, he can think what he pleases to think without regard for fact, and can act in accordance with his own reconstructions. If he chooses to regard Adam as my contractual representative, and to regard me as Adam and to hold me responsible for Adam's sin, that is his privilege, being sovereign, and it is in his power, he being omnipotent.[26] So the identification involved in the federal hypothesis is a real one, though still subjective. One should keep in mind that on this theory God does not suppose that C actually did what B did; it is only that the guilt, the legal responsibility for B's act,[27] is laid on C. C is not regarded as having actually committed the act, he is only regarded as being guilty of the act. Moses Stuart is said to have characterized this theory as one of "fictitious guilt, but veritable damnation."[28] Nevertheless, since the alleged imputation so unites B and C that A treats them alike, dealing with C as he would and does deal with B, and for the same reason, we would have to say that the identification is real, if we take the view held by the supporters of the doctrine.

The next question is: *Is it valid?* The apparent answer is, No. Such an identification is valid only when positively related to fact. There must be something in common, really in common, between B and C, at the point of the sin-and-guilt, for A's identification to be valid. No participation, no identification.

At this point an objection is in order. Do not Adam and I share one very important thing? Are we not both human? Answer to the objection: If sharing a common human nature were sufficient ground for identification, any human being could be fairly charged with the guilt of any or all other human beings; and this is absurd.

Returning to the point of participation. Proponents of the doctrine want to have it both ways. They both affirm and deny that there was participation. There was no personal participation in the act; there was no voluntary participation in the act; yet there is a participation in the sin, we are told, and/or participation in the guilt, the responsibility. Now, on what grounds is God supposed to lay on other men, as well as on Adam, the guilt of a sin which was solely Adam's? On the ground of a contractual covenant. Assuming that such a covenant had been made with Adam (of which, let it be said again, no clear Biblical evidence exists), would such a covenant be just? It does seem clear that this would have to be a three-party contract: God, Adam, and each other man. Now a contract, covenant, agreement, whatever you call it, is no contract apart from the consent of the parties concerned. I have no right to declare that a contract exists involving two other persons as principals, if either of them is ignorant of such a contract. Assuming (in the absence of any evidence to support the assumption) that Adam did consent, the question still is: Did I make such an agreement? Did Confucius make it? Did your baby make it? On the federal theory, either this was not a true agreement or covenant but an arbitrary decree, in which case we should have to talk about the truth or justice of it—or else it is a real covenant, a real agreement, in which case I, Confucius, or your baby must have made the covenant personally, which is the only way we could make it. But the plain fact is, we were not there to make the agreement. We would not have made it after the Fall; we could not have made it before the Fall. The contract is a pure fiction. It is in the same class with an accusation of conspiracy brought against a man who not only has not conspired, but who first hears of the conspiracy when arrested. The identification, being based on an impossibility, is unjustified; invalid because contrary to fact, and unjustified for the same reason. It is subjectively real but not objectively so. Now, I repeat, there is no stopping a prejudice, and a divine prejudice, if it could exist, would be the hardest of all to stop. If God were capable of forming such a prejudice we could do nothing about it; but then he would not be God.

The reason why, as appears to be the fact, the church today no longer believes in this theory, is that we believe in a God of justice and truth. So, we may say with confidence, did our forefathers. But the climate of theological opinion changes, like all mental and spiritual climates. Our forebears could in their own minds somehow reconcile belief in the justice and truth of God with belief that such a God would act in the way implied by the doctrine of imputation, as they held it. We find that more difficult today, even impossible. We believe that when we call God just and true, while the words may well point to something far greater in him than in us, the words have no meaning if they point to something quite different from or opposite to the meaning of the words as applied to us. God's justice and truth must be better than ours, not worse. A purely arbitrary deity could make such an identification as the doctrine in question alleges; an absolutely omnipotent deity could do so; but a just and true God would not, and I suspect could not. He could not, because God cannot contradict his own nature; and he would not, because he cannot even wish to contradict his own nature. The doctrine of the imputation of Adam's guilt, on the federal theory, amounts to charging God with an unfounded prejudice, a judgment made in spite of fact.

Again an objection might arise. What is the difference between falsity and make-believe? It was hinted in an earlier chapter that even God might have the right to make-believe. Has he not sovereign power here too? This, in fact, was the gist of many of the old-time defenses of this theory; God being sovereign can make any arrangements he desires, and if it is his will that all human beings should be born with a corrupt nature as a penalty for a sin they did not actually commit, then God has a right to bring this about. God has a right to treat non-existent non-sinners just as he treats one existent sinner.

The answer is simple: Not all make-believes are justified. Beautiful exhibitions of brilliant imaginative power have gone into making false alibis; but their imaginative perfection does not keep them from being lies. Furthermore, while God is sovereign, his sovereignty does not include the right to initiate his dealings with man by a tremendous falsehood.

I am not denying the sinfulness of man. I am saying that this theory of imputation is a bad way of explaining the source of his sinfulness, making it appear to be primarily the mere arbitrary will of God. I suspect that the church in general agrees with this objection, else it would hardly have left out so prominent a doctrine from its contemporary statements of belief.

It should be added that this type of imputation doctrine invites another moral objection. On this theory, the corrupt nature which man bears is an actual consequence, not primarily of his inheritance but of the imputation itself. The alleged sequence brings this out. First there is the covenant or contract by which Adam is placed on probation, with the understanding that his success or failure at one particular point will be set to the credit or the debit of each succeeding human individual. Second, there is Adam's sin, his failure to obey, with the consequent guilt entailed. Third, there is the personal, direct, immediate, penal ascription or imputation of the guilt of Adam's first sin to every human being, before birth.[29] Fourth, there is this antenatal curse, or withdrawal of grace. Fifth, is the corruption of nature, which is inborn and penal. It is the penalty for the *imputed* sin and/or guilt. Dr. A. A. Hodge says: "The imputation of the guilt of Adam's apostatizing act to us in common leads judicially to spiritual desertion in particular, and spiritual desertion leads by necessary consequence to inherent depravity."[30]

Considering the results of man's corrupt nature, we must, on these premises, regard all these bad results, the horrible sum of human evil, as the direct result of the imputation, which in turn rests on an identification. If this were a fact, we could only conclude that here is an identification which is willed, purely arbitrary, resulting in an enormous enhancement of evil, and so utterly unjustified. (All this aside from the more obvious point that it affirms what Reformed Christians as well as others deny: that God is the author of evil.) If we suppose that an identification is justified only if it enhances good and not evil, then this identification would not only not be justified, but it would be the most colossally *un*justified identification in the history of the race. Again I say, it is no wonder the Christian conscience of these times has for the most part tacitly rejected such a doctrine. It is not that we despise God or his covenant, for we know that his covenant is full of truth and grace; but the covenant we have been reviewing has the marks, as a certain Dr. Park is reported to have said, of having been made not in Eden, still less in Paradise; it was made in Holland.

Just a word now about the so-called Augustinian theory, espoused for instance by Dr. Strong and Dr. Shedd, rejected by Dr. Murray, but also at least suggested in the compound Westminster doctrine. On this theory, as in the federal theory, Adam's sin is imputed to me apart from my present knowledge and volition. This looks at first glance a good deal like the federal theory, but there is an important difference. The federal theory of imputation rests on an identification. The Augustinian theory rests on an identity. On this view, Adam's sin and mine are identical, numerically. I *did* sin in Eden. The guilt of Adam's sin is imputed to me not as a separate person but because I am the same person. The relation between the sin of all, and the sin of Adam, is not one of resemblance but of identity. There may be objections to this theory also, but they do not fall to be discussed under the head of identification. The question would be one not of fairness but of fact. The question would be: Is the identity a real one? If its reality can be accepted, there can be no argument over whether it is justified or not. A simple fact is a simple fact. For those who deny that the identity exists, one can escape into a theory involving identification, but if the identification be invalid, then other hypotheses must be tried. Into these we are not going. I have been concerned only to point to this particular doctrine as a close-home example of an unjustified identification.

4. I *Identification* in the Heart of God

We have looked into some miscellaneous theological doctrines involving the principle of identification, and have found them wanting if for no other reason than that they ignore, or make wrong use of, the principle. Now we shall try to examine some other doctrines which likewise rest on and exemplify the principle of identification. They not only involve this principle in ways both valid and justified, but they are illumined by the principle itself, sometimes to the point where a doctrine superficially obscure turns out to be full of light, and precious.

We begin with some elements in the Christian doctrine of God. We assume, until and unless we are forced to abandon the assumption, that the orthodox—that is to say, the standard, traditional main-line, ecumenical doctrine of God is true, or in the direction of truth. We assume also that the church's constructions are more than simple catenas of Scripture passages, but rather are an attempt to state the message of Scripture taken as a whole. As held in the church, the doctrine of God is a highly complex one, not only impinging on many other doctrines, but in itself including many distinct but interrelated problems. It would be impossible to deal with the whole of it, even from our purposely limited viewpoint; hence we make no attempt to be all-inclusive, but undertake only to investigate certain selected phases of the doctrine in the large.

God and Himself

First we turn to what seems most remote from practical life, most impossible (if that phrase may be pardoned) to state fully or to know clearly: namely, *God as he is in himself*. The church, on the one hand, questions the final validity of her insights here,[1] yet on the other hand has made quite definite assertions about what is surely too high for her, and yet what she is driven to think and believe despite all the compass variations and vagaries in these high regions.

If there is one dogma that is characteristically Christian, one which has the stamp of *ubique, semper et ab omnibus,* it is the doctrine of the Trinity. In spite of attacks on it ancient and modern, and in spite of the church's own confessed inability to expound the dogma both clearly and in such a way as to exclude all possibility of error—in other words, the church's inability fully to understand the doctrine she teaches—the church rightly clings to her ancient belief that God is One, and that he subsists in three Persons.

This dogma is built on data of experience and of revelation, though these two may not be sharply distinguished. Together they bear witness that God is not only knowable; he has, at least in part, been known. ("We know in part," said the Apostle; but we do know.) Our experience of God, the collective experience of the church, is given us in three ways. We know God as Father, we know God in Christ, we know him as Spirit. It appears to some that the dogma of the Trinity is a needlessly complicated way of expressing Christian religious experience. To say it more plainly: We could suppose that Father, Son, and Holy Spirit are in the last analysis words used to differentiate our experiences of God, and that beyond this we have no need to go. But the dogma or doctrine of the Trinity does make bold to go farther. In it the voice of the church affirms that there are *distinctions in deity itself* which correspond to these same distinctions in our experience of God. No one of these "persons" con-

stitutes God alone; God is constituted by all three. Yet the three
are not separate entities, not three individuals. The three are in
a relation of identity and difference, a relation which seems to
be self-contradictory and can have no explanatory parallel, yet
one which the dogma of the Trinity is designed to express or
suggest. We affirm that these distinctions and this unity are not
only in God as we know him but in God as he is; not only in
God but eternally in God. The Trinity is not the form God takes
over against this planet and its inhabitants. Over against all
possible or actual worlds, or without reference to any, God is
ever three in one and one in three.

There are two points the Christian is always instructed to remember, but can remember only by way of polar tension or paradox: namely, that the "three" do not divide the Godhead, nor
does the "one" destroy the distinctions. A better word than Trinity, in English, would be to copy the German word for it and call
it the Triunity. As Calvin says, "Let us not imagine such a trinity
of Persons, as includes an idea of separation, or does not immediately recall us to the unity."[2]

This seems confusing, but an attempt to take refuge in the
"simple words of Scripture" may confuse us even more. Some
points are clear enough. That God is One, every New Testament
writer assumes. That Father, Son, and Holy Spirit are in some
way together in that unity, is shown by such passages as ascribe
divine functions to Christ and the Holy Spirit. Dr. Warfield's
book *The Lord of Glory* goes exhaustively into this for Christ, as
long ago the *Letters Concerning the Holy Spirit* by Athanasius
collated the evidence for the deity of the Spirit.[3]

If this were all we could find, however, we might be left
with three divine beings, Father, Son, and Spirit. The New Testament will not let us be tri-theists, however. The name "GOD"
remains stubbornly singular. The identity not less than the difference, which we find in the dogma, is in the New Testament
first. We read of the judgment seat of God and of Christ;[4] of the
love of God and the love of Christ, evidently meaning the same
thing;[5] of God, or Christ, or the Holy Spirit, in the heart.[6] Yet,

that there is an irreducible, non-interchangeable distinction of Persons in the New Testament can be demonstrated by attempting to change subjects in familiar sentences and thereby coming out with statements like these: The Son sent the Father into the world . . . The Father so loved the world, that he gave the Holy Spirit, that all who believe on him might have eternal life . . . The Holy Spirit is willing to give Christ to all who ask him . . . Such parodies strike the ear harshly because they would make sense only if the relation between Father, Son, and Spirit were one of simple numerical identity.

When the young church had gone off, so to speak, to the university, it tried to put its belief into words that would be understood on a Greek campus. It came out with the well-known formula that rolls off the tongue more smoothly than it rolls into the mind: God has one *Ousia*, three *Hypostases*, or as we badly translate it, One Substance, Three Persons. One *ousia* or essence: by that they meant to say that whatever it takes to make God God, Jesus Christ has and is. One *ousia:* Whatever it takes to make the Father God, also makes the Son and Spirit God. This *Whatever* is *one;* it is a way of affirming the Identity, the self-identity of God. This unity of essence—which would still be unity if there were thirty-three persons or 33,000,000—this unity is not a bestowal, a construction, an achievement. It is not like a combination of which one could write, ". . . to form a more perfect union." The unity is always there, not growing, not diminishing, incapable of either. The affirmation is true, neither more nor less true ever since God has been God—that is to say, forever. Whatever the complexity, God is always, in time and space, or beyond, ONE.

But what is the nature of the distinctions? We have an idea of the difference between Father, Son, and Holy Spirit in Christian experience, but what of these distinctions in the inner and ultimate and eternal Being of God? One thing is certain, we cannot explain them. God can be explained only to himself and by himself, not by me to you or vice versa. However, if the distinctions like the unity are just left to float in space like Echo

I, riddled with meteorites of unanswered questions, a bare and barren mystery; if all we can say about the distinction of persons is that they are distinct, not exactly modes of existence, pure and simple, and not exactly like individual persons pure and simple; if all we can say about their "properties" is that the Father begets but is not begotten, that the Son is begotten but does not proceed, and the Spirit proceeds but is not begotten, or that the Father's special property is generation, the Son's is filiation, and the Spirit's is spiration,[7] then we are left with an ontological doctrine of God which is metaphysically mystifying and morally meaningless. If all we have, and all we can say, is that God has his being in indivisible unity combined in whatever intelligible or unintelligible fashion with hypostatic distinctions, then indeed we have a doctrine of the Trinity which may wisely be left to professional and incurable hair-splitters.[8]

Into this darkness the principle of identification, especially as linked with that of identity, may cast some light. I submit that in the Trinity, even though full understanding is ever beyond us, we are privileged to contemplate the supreme example of identity and identification, conjoined and mutually self-supporting. Identification, in our world, may sometimes involve a game of make-believe. Possibly this is so even when God does it; but not here. Identity also may become a kind of game; but not here. We are confronted, in the Trinity, by the most thoroughgoing and genuine identity and identification, and both at the most sublime degree.

First, *identity*. In spite of all the efforts to de-Hellenize theology, and the restoration of a less metaphysical exegesis of Exodus 3:14, "He who Is" remains a basic way of denominating God. If you cannot take it from Exodus, you may take it from Second Isaiah: "I am the Lord, and there is no other, besides me there is no God" (Isaiah 45:5). Only God can affirm identity as he does. He alone is almighty, for he alone IS. The same unique, irreproducible, indefectible BEING is the Being of the entire Trinity. If the Godhead be, as Dr. Richardson suggests, incalculably plural, unimaginably complex, infinitely profound, this ineffable and complex essence is nevertheless single and identical. The identity is not reduced by the distinction of persons, nor belied by them. If there were two essences there would be two Gods.

Like all true identities, moreover, this one is a numerical identity. Here is a paradox. We have said that every identity is numerical; yet as will be said, the Persons of the Trinity are not numerically identical, and yet they are so. The church has never said, in fact, that they are identical; rather, that their *essence* is identical. This is awkward, and we do not escape all difficulty by resorting to the categories of identification and identity. There is no explaining God! If anything, the use of these categories only sharpens the paradox of the Infinite; and yet they are not unfruitful, even so. Provisionally, the identity of essence among the Persons of the Trinity may be thought of as a simple fact, something even God has to accept. If this seems a rash speculation, let us admit that what we are doing is speculative, but done in a spirit of reverence, not without reason and not without faith. We have high company—Anselm and Aquinas and all who have tried to see some pattern in what is given us from Above. As for there being something necessary about God, there have been theologians who declared that everything about him is necessary; he is even defined as the Most Necessary Being.[9]

But something more needs to be said. It will be remembered that five types of identification were distinguished, the fifth type being one of two (4 and 5) which involve an identity. In this Type A, who being A cannot be non-A, knows this and rejoices in the fact. Brute fact it may be. Given in the nature of things, or rather in the nature and will of God, it may be; and as such has to be accepted. The only alternatives to acceptance are refusal to think about it at all, ignoring it, or denying it outright—reactions choosing falsehood rather than truth. But even acceptance can be of more than one kind. It can be resentful, it can be dull and disinterested, or it can be voluntary and joyous. Applied to the Trinity, I suggest that this means that Father, Son, and Spirit *will—choose*, if you like—to be one in essence. At this point, picking up the difference between the modal and the societal conceptions of the Trinity, on the former hypothesis we would say simply that God chooses to be single in essence, as he is. On the latter hypothesis, we would say that God in each of his centers of consciousness chooses to be single in essence, as he is.[10] From the one point of view it can be said that God's mind assents with unshaken good will to the given fact of identity. From the other point of view it can be said that the minds of God's three Persons rejoice as one in the fact of identity.

One finds it distasteful to say that anything about God is something he cannot help. That is why it causes some unease to be told that (for example) the generation of the Son is a necessary act, something God eternally does because he eternally must. However, if we grant that there are necessities in the life and being of God, and if we grant that one of the necessities is his unity of essence, there still can be, and I believe there is, a high, supernally moral quality both about the unity and about God's joy in it. As theologians put it, God's concomitant will approves his necessary will. Some human beings seem to be uneasy at having to *be* human. But we cannot think of God as somewhat uneasy at having to be God! He is what he wants to be and he wants to be what he is. We need not inquire whether the joy of God is threefold or single; whether it belongs to the Persons as the older theology might have thought, or to the essence, as Bishop Aulén might think. What we have a right to believe is that God, as Father, Son, and Spirit, never in the least degree strains away from himself; never do the Persons of the Trinity take one another for granted. They rejoice actively that they are one.

Now consider the difference or distinction in the "Persons." As has been indicated, when it is said that these distinctions are ontological, what is meant is that these are not merely names for the modes by which we apprehend God. He is not a Fourth Something behind Father, Son, and Spirit. The God who comes to us, the God we know in each of the ways of knowing him, is the same God. We have been saying that the identity expressed in the phrase "one substance" is numerical, for there is no other kind. And yet, if anything is clear from the New Testament, there is *no* numerical identity among Father, Son, and Spirit, as such. A study of the passages in Paul or John where Christ and the Father are most closely associated—that is, the pre-incarnate Christ, the eternal Logos—will show that they would not make sense if the same word God, or Son, is used for both. Take any of the great Christological passages and read them using the same name. You come out with irrationalities such as "Christ sat down at his own right hand," "I have not yet ascended unto myself," and so on. Still less can you reverse the names, as you may in a case of numerical identity. You cannot (for example) make Paul write, "Then shall God also himself be subject . . . that the Son may be all in all."[11] This is plainly nonsense.

Must we not suppose that the Persons of the Trinity, however they subsist, rejoice in their distinctiveness as surely as they rejoice in their unity? But if no more can be said than this, then we might suppose that our metaphysical puzzle pointed to an actual divine fact, a very disturbing one: namely, that in God there must be a kind of straining against himself, after all. For there would be a nisus toward unity in the essence, a nisus toward divergence in the Persons. Is there any way, suggested by the Bible itself, some way in which the threeness supports the oneness instead of pulling against it, and the unity is maintained even in and by the distinctiveness?

There is a way—in this principle of *identification*. It is not possible here to examine all the Christological passages, much less all those referring to the Spirit. I would simply say that the New Testament suggests this very principle of identification in the Trinity, in the forms already suggested as 2 and 3. It is often expressed by the simple preposition *in*. "Thou, Father, art in me, and I in thee" were Jesus' words. This is hinted at in the Prologue to John, where the Logos is said to be *"pros* ton theon"; not merely "with" God but at home with God, related to God, literally speaking *toward* God. Identification, we said, is an act of will. It does not create identity, it is not identity; but it does create unity. This is not saying that the unity of God grows with the years. It *is* saying that the unity of God is more than a simple numerical singleness, it is more than identity of essence, even where that identity subsists dynamically and is accepted with gladness. The unity of God is the mutual and eternal self-giving of each person to each other "person," it is the movement of each "toward" the other, the merging of each "in" the other without losing separate identity.

The unity of God is thus seen to be more than a given fact. It is a moral fact at the highest level, which is to say that it is a holy fact. The unity of God is not alone to be recognized, it is to be praised. The unity of God is in its fullness a reflection of the character of God, an expression of the love of God.[12]

If this is essentially true, then the western Christian world is surely right in affirming the double procession of the Spirit. The formula is stylized and stiff; but the spirit of it is true. The Eastern Orthodox formula omitting the *Filioque* leaves the impression that the Spirit comes from the Father with the Son as it were a bystander, interested but not active. Even when the revised formula is used, that the Spirit comes from the Father through the Son, one still has the impression that the Son is passive, or secondary at best. It is when we think of the Spirit as coming from both Father and Son that we have that in-ness of each in the other, that full identification, which is moral to the core.

The principle of identification, furthermore, is far more dynamic than simple unity of essence, and nearer the truth than doctrines of circumincession and perichoresis. When we speak of God's attributes as being identical in Father, Son, and Spirit, we are not only running the risk of making the unity mechanical, or affirming identity instead of identification, we are tending to impersonalize the unity. Thinking in terms of identification helps the Christian to think of the unity of God in a personal rather than an impersonal way. Not to think in this way leaves us with a God whose unity is metaphysical, non-moral, a God whose activities may be personal but whose basic and essential unity is not personal at all. But if in God there is not only metaphysical unity of essence, accepted and rejoiced in, but also the moral unity of a complete, unqualified three-way identification, then the unity not less than the triunity is holy. It is not a new idea that the Persons of the Trinity interpenetrate one another; but this is not by a kind of celestial osmosis whereby attributes slip like a ghostly virus through the meshes of the filter dividing hypostasis from hypostasis. We cannot peer into what forever lies beyond us; we should not dare to set up a kind of mechanism of trinity to which God must conform. Just as at the entrance to certain vital areas the visitor must leave his camera behind, so at the portal of eternal mysteries the worshiper should leave his drawing board outside. Still, we can dare to believe that the triunity of God is far more nearly analogous to the interfusion of personalities through love, than it is to any capillary transfer of matter, or to the logical identities among various modes or aspects of the divine subsistence. God is He, not They, not It. In this simple grammar the church affirms her personal faith in the personal God whose inner distinctions are personal, and whose inner life, infinitely and ineffably more complex, we may be sure, than the complexities of our own souls, and yet more profoundly One, is personal in every particle and purpose. With the light cast by the principle of identification, the divine Triunity may still be beyond our understanding, but not beyond our praise. We have a right to sing the Doxology, not a Paradoxology. Far be it from any man to probe into the inner secrets of the Unrevealed. But God's revelation of himself as Father, Son, and Spirit, seen as the supreme and perfect mutual identification, shows to us the basis and beginning of that which comes to us as God's redeeming love.

God and the Cosmos

We come now to a question which should be easier than the question of God's internal relations, that is to say with and within himself: namely, his relations with other

existences. Let us admit that we do not know what other existences there are. What unimaginable universes may have existed,
may now exist, or may emerge into existence in future aeons,
"cosmic epochs," no man knows and it has not been shown to us.
What we do know, just a little, is the cosmos. This is a conven-
ient word to cover the whole of existence excepting God:[13] this
"sorry scheme of things entire," as Omar Khayyam put it, or this
glorious scheme, this best of all possible worlds, as more optimistic philosophers like Leibnitz and Hocking might say. By
cosmos is to be understood not only nature in the sense of physical objects—worms, elephants, planets, stars—not only matter
in all forms past, present, or future, but the forms and patterns
themselves, the so-called "laws" which science discovers—cosmic habits, if you like, which the scientist describes. By cosmos
is meant also all other forms of existence besides material,
especially what we call variously mind and spirit; all that is, in
short, that is not God. The question is: *Is God identified with
the cosmos* in any way and to any degree? We must recognize,
without trying to refute, alternative views which would elimi-
nate the question as meaningless, or would offer a different
answer from that to be proposed here. There are atheists, seldom
claiming that designation, who find no need for the hypothesis
of God in their life and profession: not only atomic scientists,
economists, rocket men, computer men, but also men in the
"humane" professions—lawyers, teachers, and others; not all of
these, of course, but such of them as see no force nor reality beyond nature, dealing with mind as a part of nature, including also
those philosophers of language who cannot find even meaning,
whether true or false, in affirmations regarding God. These all
must regard our immediate question as meaningless, and the
appeal to superhuman values or purposes, or forces, as a waste
of time. Such persons have no answer to our question, for the
question itself is regarded as illegitimate.

The Deists had an answer. "Had," because they are not around
any more, chiefly for the reason that in our present world few if
any can be found to join the Bolingbroke-Pope duet, "Whatever is,

is right." The Deists' answer would have been that God's intentions were so precisely carried out in creation that all one has to do is to scrutinize the cosmos and there observe a transcription, undefaced, of the mind and will of God. The place of the Deists as the optimistic wing of Christianity has been taken by the pantheists, who can sing Pope's refrain, "Whatever is, is right," by emphasizing the word IS. Whatever is not right, or seems not to be right, simply *is not*, it has no reality except the shadowy reality of a hallucination. The pantheist, current style, does not see a relation of identification between God and the world, but sees rather a relation of identity. There is one very significant difference, however: In God there is no error, while in the cosmos there is an embarrassing amount of it. In the cosmos, as reinterpreted by the pantheist, God is seen with the eye of faith, directly and clearly. If clarity be lacking, the dimness is in our eyes, not in God nor in the creation which is one with him.

Then there is the view, widely held and supplanting the older orthodoxy in many places, the view associated with the name of Karl Barth. It is impossible to be fair to a doctrine one does not fully understand; but as I see it, it amounts to saying, There is no revelation outside Christ, or outside the Bible in its totality as the living Word. Associated with this view is one that goes farther in denigrating nature. God is said to have laid all nature (namely, the universe) under a curse.[14] Now it is easy to understand that man's evil ways, or merely his shortsighted, lazy, negligent ways, have in many times and places laid waste this fair green earth. But man has not brought a curse to everything he has touched. He certainly did not bring a curse upon the wild rose when he developed the Maréchal Neil, nor despoil the wild creatures he tamed for his use and pleasure. Furthermore, it is difficult to know just what would be the difference between a blue sky under a curse and the same sky with the curse lifted. How is a violet cursed different from a violet blessed? At all events, on this view there can be no talk of God's identification with the cosmos. The Almighty threw it into existence by an act of will; that some kind of cosmos there should be, he planned; but that *this* cosmos should be what and as it is, is not his design. The alleged handwriting of God in nature is all forgeries. The identification of God with nature, in any sense, is close to blasphemy.

Against this view is an older one, perhaps still the majority view in Christendom. It is, in brief, that God is sufficiently identified with the cosmos that in it and by its light we can know something true about God—not everything, not enough for salvation, but some basic truths.

God and the world are over against each other, but not therefore discontinuous. Nature does not offer us a path that leads all the way to God, but does set us in a path that leads toward him. It must be admitted, of course, that nature taken alone does not speak with a clear and single voice. There are many contradictions in nature: the butterfly and the tiger, the breeze and the hurricane, the beneficence of fire, and its terror. Those who have erected their altars by the light of nature alone have bowed to some very strange gods. The handwriting of God can be misread, but it is his all the same.

Now the identification of God with the cosmos must be of Type 3 as we distinguished it. The true identification of God with the cosmos cannot be made by men, it cannot be made by the cosmos. It can only be made by God himself. Except for the pantheist it cannot be Type 4 or 5, because these involve discovery or recognition of identity, and this is ruled out for all Christians. God is always other than his world. The identification of God with his world is not conceivably of the type in which one person seeks to be identified with another, even to the point, in extreme cases, of willingness to surrender one's own identity and be lost in that of the Other. This would involve God in a sort of worship of his own handiwork. He called it good, but not better than himself.

If identification there be, it must be of Type 3, where the identifier desires the identified to *be* identified with *him*. We said that this type is usually harmful, for as practiced between man and man, or parent and child, it eats out the personality of the identified. But it is not bad when God is the identifier. On first thought, it would seem that the very nature of creation precludes identification. For at base, the doctrine of creation is the affirmation that *God willed that something should be that is not he*.[15] This basic truth underlies all the others that cluster here. The universe is not God in disguise, not partly God, not God without remainder, not God's body, not God at all. And yet there is identification. The only way to deny this while maintaining the doctrine of creation would be to suppose that God forsook his creation, or laid it under a curse. This the Bible as a whole does not support.

We might ask a question such as the medieval scholars pondered: Could God create anything which makes no sense, and is entirely anti-God in its very existence? From the viewpoint of God's absolute omnipotence, the answer might be yes, though it would involve a logical contradiction; but from the viewpoint that God's omnipotence is *his* omnipotence, of a piece with his entire holy being, he could not create such an object, for to do so would involve him in cross-purposes, in self-contradiction. He would be like a man in a new house, bringing in a bug to step on.

Granted this much, i.e., if we cannot conceive of God as *creating* what is not good, or what is utterly foolish, we can see a fair answer to the question, In what way may the universe be identified with God? (We have already ruled out identity.) It may surely be identified with God's *mind*. If we take the doctrine of creation seriously, then the existence of the cosmos *überhaupt* represents God's will and intent. As against Buddhist and similar faiths, the Christian faith declares that not non-being but *being* is the central will of God. We do not honor God, we slander him, by seeking release from existence. In itself, existence is nothing that interferes with and thwarts God. Existence is not a tricky and troublesome lock that keeps us out of the secrets of God. It is rather an open vista into the intent of God. To be, to help to be, to contribute to being, is Godlike; to wish not to be, to damage and belittle what God has made, to thwart and dwarf and limit being, is anti-God.

Not bare existence per se but the structures also of the cosmos are part of God's identification with it. From this standpoint distinctions between natural and supernatural are somewhat dubious. That 2 and 2 do not make 5 is not a natural nor a supernatural fact exclusively. It is not something God was forced to accept. When he created the universe, he created it with all its numerical and logical structures; these, too, are part of his plan. The law of the undistributed middle is a divine law as much as any law of physics, or of the Ten Commandments.

It is hard to see how it can be thought that *nothing* of the divine mind can be found in the cosmos. For at every point, as human minds explore the universe around us, regularities, consistencies, uniformities are discovered. The universe, as James Jeans said, begins to look more like a great thought than like a great machine. What mind can discern bears evidence of mind in its making. It cannot be said that this conclusion solves all the logical and moral puzzles of this fantastic universe. But to those who will listen, the being of the world, and the beauty and the order of the world, do speak of the creative mind of One who flung all this against the night.

One would think that Christians would not make this harder to believe. But a special difficulty is raised by that most popular of all religious convictions, belief in Providence. This doctrine affirms that not only does God create all things, he also maintains all things. He not only willed them into being, he presently and continuously wills their being. The doctrines of Creation and Providence are usually taught as expressions of one truth. Without his will and power, any thing or all things would vanish as an unremembered dream. Especially in the Reformed churches, the doctrine of Providence is an all-inclusive one. God is personally and actively present at every point of space and time. He is associated with trifles like a sparrow's fall, as well as with the most stupendous events, the rise and fall of empires, the loss or saving of human souls. There is a familiar difficulty here. If God's nature or essence is love, how can he be associated with, much less identified with, that wherein no love is to be discerned? The church has never solved that problem—our creed leaves the unanswerable questions unanswered. But she would cling to the doctrine of Providence rather than believe what is implied in abandoning it. The doctrine of Providence makes it possible to see some identification of history with the purposes of God. More personally, it makes it possible to believe that whether or not he fixes in advance the occurrence of all that occurs, the cosmos will not slip from his control.

To sum up: Accepting the identification of the universe with the intention of God leads to the conclusion that it is God's intention that the universe itself shall more and more embody and cast light on the mind and the purpose of God.

We say "more and more" because that appears to be the teaching of the Bible. This is the truth in the doctrine of the curse on nature. It has been wrongly supposed that because God looked on all that he had made and called it good, he thereby called it perfect. The imperfection of the cosmos, imperfection in the sense of improvability, is suggested by the command given to Adam: Replenish the earth—and subdue it. The corner of the cosmos accessible to man is an unfinished creation. Man's use of it, according to God's first intention, is to be such as to bring out more fully, indeed to fulfill, the purposes of creative Love. Thus the identification of God with the "humbler creation" is not complete, and cannot be, apart from man.

If a practical application is desired, our church has made one. Our creed enjoins the reverent use of all that represents (or, in our category, is identifiable with) God: specifically, his word and his works. To let "nature" deteriorate, as in careless strip-mining; to permit preventable erosion of the soil, or to neglect one's own health, for example, are species of irreverence. One can find this viewpoint in the Bible. The prophet Zechariah looks forward to an earthly paradise when even the bells on the horses' harness shall be inscribed, "Holy to the LORD" (Zechariah 14:20). "Be holy, for I am holy" is a refrain recurrent in one of the ancient codes having to do with human relationships (Leviticus 11:44). Jesus rebuked those who were too proper to swear by God, but swore by the gold on the Temple, or by the earth; such swearing was irreverent, for all these were somehow identified with God. It would amount to an ethical revolution if we took this thought seriously and began to think of "our neighbor the universe"[16] less as treasure to be plundered than as actually carrying the holiness, and potentially the purpose, of the Creator of all.

God's Relations with Man

We have thought, not without difficulty, of God's identifications within his own being, and over against his universe. (So long as we call it *his* universe we betray some expectation of identification!) A problem more existential but not for that reason any whit easier, is the question of God's identification with man. As is well known, there is a view held by western thinkers, and perhaps tenable only in western culture as it has recently flowered, that makes the relation of God and man one of identity, only not in the pantheist manner. God disappears; man becomes the only god there is. The humanist does not like to be called an atheist. He is only an a-theist.[17] God's relation to man or relations with him cannot, of course, be discussed by the humanist. Pantheism also sees an identity of God and man. Deists could not; which may be set to their credit.

The relation of God to man cannot be fully discussed apart from Christ. It cannot be comprehended until the present great gap in our knowledge has been filled in, namely, the life of man beyond the line of death. So here we must confine ourselves to two preliminary questions. Full answers would fill and do fill many books; we are asking only about the principle of identification. (1) Is it involved in God's relation to and relations with "man by creation," that is, man by God's first intention? (2) What of God's relations with man as sinner?

Here we come for a second time to a special kind of identification, one which is reciprocal. As maintained within the Trinity, we considered that this is purely and perfectly reciprocal and mutual, each outreach meeting equal response. In

love, says a French proverb, there is one who kisses and one who
offers the cheek. This is a somewhat cynical phrasing of a truth
about human relationships; they are seldom if ever totally reciprocal, or symmetrical. Now God originally intended that man
should be identified with him, in a way that could not be true of
the cosmos. The cosmos cannot consciously respond to God; man
can. Indeed, many thinkers limit the meaning of "image of God"
to simple capacity for response.[18] In this writer's judgment, the
matter goes deeper than that; but let it rest here for a moment.
If we follow the hints of Genesis 1 and 2, man is expected to
complete and carry on the work of God. He is to remember that
he is a creature, though he is not placed beyond the possibility
of temptation to imagine himself more than a creature. But *as*
a creature, as the top of the pyramid of life on earth, as the one
special creature, his assigned destiny is to carry on God's purposes in himself and for the earth from which and on which he
lives. Then comes the story of the Fall—the parable-story of
how man chose to be identified with anti-God, not with God.
Incredible, inexplicable. Seeing it come to pass again and in
ourselves, a thousand times, may make it more credible; but
the mystery remains. Now what happened here? Or what happens here when it happens in you? The reciprocity of identification has been rejected. In the formal terms of our diagram, God's
intention is for man's identification with *him*, whereas man's
basic sin is that he wants to turn this around. He wants God to
be identified with *him*. Instead of being drawn in or drawn up-
ward to God's purpose, vision, destiny, man desires that God
shall be drawn down as chief assistant and guarantor of man's
schemes, plans, and desires. Do not all religious persons believe
in God? Yet how many of these believe in God for irreligious
reasons? Man does not want to be identified with God in purpose.[19]

　　Not only so, but the Fall involved and involves a rejection
of the image of God.[20] This raises a most important question:
What happened to the image of God? Is it gone entirely, is it un-
damaged, or is it somewhere in between, damaged yet not past

recognition? For present purposes, it makes no great difference whether we take as a clue to the meaning of the "image" the notion of response, or responsibility, or the Genesis hint of similarity. Sin apart, the image of God would have been the outstanding, the glorious feature of man.

Yet man has rejected it so stubbornly that in man, as sinner, the very existence of this image is often denied. And small wonder. Yet the Bible testifies, or at any rate some writers in the Bible testify, to its continuance. Offenses against man are reckoned as offending God. Cain settled scores with Abel quite simply, he thought. He drew a bloody finger across the page. The balance was struck. But he had not reckoned with God. Murder was forbidden for many reasons, but one given long before the time of the Law is that murder is an attack on the image of God.

God's chosen people always had one chronic blind spot. They could not see what they had in common with the rest of mankind. They had difficulty regarding their contemporaries outside Israel as persons, still less as persons of interest to God. The very existence of pagans was a puzzle. The heathen— pardon the language—"are nothing and are like spittle."[21] Yet the prophets read God's intentions otherwise, and, we believe, read them aright. God's identification-of-concern went farther than the people thought. "Israel will be the third with Egypt and Assyria," said Isaiah (19:24). God brought the Philistines from Caphtor, as much as the Israelites from Egypt, Amos said (9:7). Jonah's God, if not Jonah, could be distressed over a pagan city that had never meant any good toward Israel. Malachi sees a pure sacrifice being offered to God in many lands outside Palestine, by many others than the "Holy People" (Malachi 1:11). So, even if dimly and occasionally, there were inspired minds able to see across high and heavy barriers the common humanity of men, and the concern of God for all.

Yet there is a deeper level, and we must be aware of it, though it cannot be brightly illumined. God has a concern for men, for some men. This is not too hard to believe, especially for a believer who counts himself among the "some." God has a concern for *all* men. This is much harder to believe. Must we, can we, believe that the desires of God are frustrated? If God has a desire that all men shall be drawn unto him, he meets frustration in the indifference or spite which most men show toward him. How can it be that God has a concern for all men? Is it that he is the cosmic chess player and we his pawns? A player is concerned for every one of his pawns. But when the game is won, he sweeps the pawns, queen, king, the whole apparatus of the game, back into the box. Is history a vast chessboard on which, for reasons of his own, God wants some personal victory? Are we pawns and no more? On the contrary, even in the Old Testament we find such an astonishing statement as: "In all their affliction *he* was afflicted" (Isaiah 63:9). If this referred to great saints, we could more readily believe it; but the prophet says it of sinful Israel. The prophet is aware of the paradox. He says God "turned to be their enemy, and himself fought against them"; yet presently says, "Thou, O Lord, art our Father, our Redeemer from of old . . ." (Isaiah 63:10, 16). Here we are in the presence of a mystery: the divine and almighty Father distressed by evil not of his doing, contrary to his will, fighting against his chosen people; and yet though he allows his people to be swept by the whirlwinds of retribution, he is no less a Father, no less concerned.[22]

Here comes out clearly what was not so clear before: this identification of God with man, this desire to mold men to his own character and purpose, is the identification of love. This tireless, ageless, unswerving will that man shall be Godlike, really Godlike and not playing God; that man shall respond to God's yearning with desire of his own, however weak it be; this persistence of God's concern for people who reject him— this is indeed a mystery. Have we come at last to an actual divine make-believe? Does God conceal his failures from himself, does he pretend, like some rejected lovers, that he has not really been rejected? Is his identification with man—rather, his desire for man's identification with him—a kind of habit, carried on after it has proved its uselessness? Or is there a kind of divine rationality about this? Does God's persistence make sense, is there any logic in it?

Only the logic of love. For love believes all things, hopes all things, endures all things. Why this can be true of God is a question no man can answer, except to say, that is the kind of God he is. What we know is, that what for us is profoundest mystery, is at the same time what we must, desperately must, believe.

5. I The *Identifications* of Christ

If we have kept together so far, we have seen that God does not exist, he is not revealed, except by some form of identification. We may therefore expect identification in what is alleged to be divine. It would not be true to say that wherever there is identification, there is evidence of deity, for as already hinted, identification can be futile and even fiendish. On the other hand, where God is alleged to be, there identification is to be expected. No identification, no God.

This is supremely and centrally true of Jesus Christ. In him we come on to the very heart of the Christian faith. If our faith is centered in Christ it is centered in God; if it is centered in God it cannot bypass Christ. When the church tries to express, concretely, what she means by "divine," she always points to Christ. On the other hand, when the church tries to express what she means by man, again she points to Christ. While the formulas of Chalcedon do not satisfy most Protestant thinkers today, the faith which those formulas were designed to express is still the faith of the Christian church, as an examination of contemporary Christologies will show.[1] Christ, so the church affirms, is God, is man, is One.

When we turn our attention now to the identifications of Christ, meaning by that his self-identifications, are we still speaking of the identifications of God? Or are we speaking of the identifications made by the man Christ Jesus? The matter will become clearer as we go on. It will help to clarify our thinking if we indicate the total scope of his identifications in the following short outline:

The Identifications of—
  (1) The Eternal Christ.
  (2) The Historic Christ.
  (3) The Risen Christ.

The Eternal Christ:
The Incarnation

The historic Christ would never have existed, as the Christ, if it had not been for the primal identifications of the Eternal Christ. We can begin from any one of three key sentences in the New Testament. "God . . . gave his only Son . . ." "Christ Jesus, . . . though he was in the form of God, did not count equality with God a thing to be grasped, but emptied himself, taking the form of a servant, being born in the likeness of men. And being found in human form he humbled himself . . ." and returning to John's simplicity again: "The Word was with God, and the Word was God. . . . And the Word became flesh" (John 3:16; Philippians 2:5-8; John 1:1, 14). Each one of these sentences implies the strangest identification of all, yet the central one in the range of Christian faith. They imply *the will and the intention on the part of God to identify himself with man.* It is the identification, or identifications, involved in the Incarnation. When we come to this, we are still forced to struggle with words that point beyond all possible realms of comprehensible meaning to regions of ever-resistant light. If we cannot prescribe methods of operation to the Triunity, we are equally fenced in by human limitations when we speak of what went on behind the veil of the Incarnation. The Incarnation is like the bursting of a wall, the sudden shearing of a veil in two . . . We can see with our own eyes and our hands can handle that which emerges. We can say, or some can say, We have beheld his glory. But of what went on before the Incarnation, on the far side of it, we can only pursue such hints as the New Testament offers. We can follow Mary on her journey from Nazareth to Bethlehem, but who can follow the journey of the Logos of God from eternity into time?

The how of it, we may be thankful, is not our concern. What is our concern is the truth of it. Granted the truth of it, some of its implications are not beyond reasonable surmise. This, I repeat, is the central, vital point in Christian faith, the crucial instance of identification between God and man. The Incarnation was neither an accident nor an event which logically had to be. It is represented in the New Testament always as a free occurrence. Theologians have long debated the necessity of the Incarnation, and, if it was necessary, whether the necessity roots in God's original design for the cosmos and the race of man, or in the desperate sinfulness of man. Either way, it is represented as God's decision, not man's (John 1:13); and we have a right to believe that God's high decisions are free from any necessity outside his own being.

First of all, if what was said in the preceding chapter is sound, some identification between God and man was not first actualized at Bethlehem. The over-against-ness of God and his creatures, all his creatures, does not prevent but rather makes possible whatever identifications there are. From the time in the unimaginable past when first the image of God could be descried in the first man—from Eden to Bethlehem—God, whose very self is not his self apart from the Logos, had been eternally Expression, outreach, relation. The Word became flesh, but the Word had always become. The Word became the order of the cosmos, where the galaxies wheel their vast splendors against the night, where the innumerable suns rise "rank on rank, the army of unalterable law."[2] The Word had become the reason and the conscience of man. Without the Logos man would have been as a beast, with neither conscience nor reason. The starry heavens above and the moral law within, not to speak of the beauty of the world that was not less beautiful when there was no human eye to see—all bespoke the majesty and power of the Creator God. He was indeed identified with his creation in various ways. He was even identified, as we have noted, so far with man that the affliction of his people, his vacillating unfaithful people, was an affliction to him as well.

Yet the Incarnation involved something new. This was an identification different from all that went before, all that came after. All that went before climaxed here, all that comes after begins here. Every statement in the New Testament affirming or implying the Incarnation points in the same direction as those key sentences already quoted. This, for instance: "God shows his love for us in that while we were yet sinners Christ died for us" (Romans 5:8).

This is our principle of identification, in action from God to man. In terms of our definition, this was an act involving understanding and will, relating two personal subjects numerically different—and here we must say as different as it is possible to be —in such a way that they are regarded and treated in all possible respects as the same. God, by his own self-emptying, can be, and wishes to be, regarded and treated for this decisive moment as in all possible respects the same as man.

It has become somewhat the fashion to say that the whole Trinity was incarnate.[3] It might be better to say with a more ancient accent that the Son of God, the One who being in the form of God thought being equal with God not a thing to be grasped—the Logos, the Son who was before Abraham—that he was incarnate; but that the Triunity, by virtue of that same interfusion of dynamic will which constitutes the divine inner self-identification—the whole Triunity was there active. In John's Gospel, Jesus says "I came" or "I was sent." Either proposition, in the divine light, implies the other. As for the Spirit, there is the thrice-told story of the Dove coming just at the day and hour when Jesus first almost dramatically, even shockingly, identified himself with the worst of men.

The Incarnation was real. If the Gospels teach us anything it is that. The flesh which the Logos became was real flesh. Our forefathers perceived that. But they were thinking more narrowly than we have to think. For them, as they argued against the Docetists, the great point was that Jesus was *physically* a real man. Today, against the Docetists in the church, it has to be argued that Christ was *mentally* and *spiritually* a man; not a kernel of impassible deity in a shell of humanity, nor yet a man transformed into a God, but a real man, wholly man. A Christ who could look like a man and talk like a man, bleed and perspire and grow weary and die like a man, yes; but unless he also thought and suffered in mind and doubted, unless he was capable of surprise, of horror and shock, he was not a man but a mask. Yes, our Lord identified himself with man—not only with the appearance of man, not with the bones and blood of a man, but with man within and without; not only the fragile weary body as our forefathers saw, but the fragile weary soul, and a heart that could be hurt. (Dare we say also a soul that could be lost?) The will to identification surely goes farther than the wish to appear what one is not. Some heretics, and some who pass for orthodox, represent the Incarnation as if it were an adventure, incognito, on the part of Omnipotence, amounting to no more than the Divine pretending to be human. But this is no divine make-believe. God must be taken with the utmost seriousness here if anywhere. Identification is more than taking on the shell of that with which one is to be identified—taking the name, the appearance, the reputation. The mere wish to be taken for someone else has very little significance. Children, actors, and criminals specialize in this. But it is not identification. God will not play at Incarnation any more than at Atonement. So the Incarnation was real, desperately real. It was real because it was willed by the God of truth, the God who never wills the unreal; the God who may tell the truth in story form but never truth in form of lies.

If we may pursue our analysis somewhat farther, we might ask about the type of this identification. Is this what we have called Type 2, the identification of devotion, in which the identifier strives to identify himself with the identified, or is it Type 3, the in-drawing kind, in which the identifier strives to identify the identified with himself? The answer must be: It is both. It is a unique type, the identification of love. "Love" of the narrow, self-seeking kind, the common parody on love, shows, as a main characteristic, identification of Type 3, reaching out to pull the other one into identification with the self, one personality eating out and (as it were) eating up another. If to gain this end the identifier shows some trace of Type 2—that is, if there is some outgoing, some devotion—that is nothing more than a temporary device, for the easier fulfillment of the other self-feeding devotion.

But the identification of which we are now speaking, our Lord's identification with man, is a manifestation of God's love, not self-seeking. It is not a parody. Can we not say that only God can justifiably will an identification of the in-drawing kind, only God can justifiably will and intend to draw others into himself? For only God has pure and unalloyed *Agape* love. Man may have it in part, does have it, cannot find his destiny without it; yet it is invariably colored, stained, tinged, and tainted even if never so slightly, so that even in the purest, rarest human form, there is still something of self-seeking in identification of this indrawing kind.

We may admit, verbally, that both God and the selfish hypocrite have this in common: They exercise identification of Type 2, the devotional type, as a means of realizing identification of Type 3, the in-drawing type. But the resemblance can be shocking only till we remember that it is merely verbal. For the motive of an identification is a criterion by which it is to be judged as justified or unjustified. The motive of the hypocrite is pure self-aggrandizement. The motive of God is pure *Agape* love. For the identified, the hypocrite has only contempt or ill-will. For the identified, God has only concern for his good. The identifier of evil intent feeds and fattens himself on the self-immolation of his devoted victims, like every fat tyrant since society began. On the contrary, the divine desire that man be identified with *Him* passes the test: *Herein is love.*

The Historic Christ:
Incarnation and Atonement

So much for the high intent of God, which cannot be dissevered from the intent of the Eternal Christ. How was it fulfilled?

The beginning of the fulfillment of that identification, it is often said, took place at Bethlehem. But shall we not say that the fulfillment, not less than the intent, was earlier, far earlier? Paul says that Christ was born in the fullness of time. This is not an arbitrary date, but the ripe moment of completion of a historical sequence, which like all other sequences is not alone, but is connected at every point with all the other happenings in the world. Fulfillment was in the baby that took Cain's place; in the little childless family that survived the Flood, and also in the cousins who perished in it; in Abraham and his family, but also in the Canaanites and Egyptians and others who were the molds through which that family found shape. The identification of God embodied in the Incarnation was no second thought for God, nor was the fulfillment a sudden call to the Angel Gabriel to share a new-made plan with Mary. Plan and accomplishment, purpose and fulfillment, were in God's weaving room long before being shown to human eye. Indeed, we have reason to believe that plan and intention, the vast Design, was in the mind of God before ever it was woven in the loom of time. Be that as it may, the personal, individual, and perfect fulfillment of this great and central identification of love, we may say, began at Bethlehem. This child, this boy, young man, carpenter (or farmer?), teacher, preacher, healer, friend, calling himself a man yet Son of God, like unto his brothers in all respects, sin apart: he now had his own identifications to make. If he had not made them and made them as he did, the intention of God in the all-embracing identification of prevenient love would, so far as we can see, have gone awry. The identifications of Jesus were often misread. His own mother's famous song, compared with subsequent history or with Jesus' own expressed intentions, for all its beauty sounds like a sort of narrow parody of what actually came true. He was misunderstood to and beyond the moment of his death. As he sank to the last heartbeat he could hear the taunt: He saved others; himself he cannot save. Words were thrown at him like a rebuke: Save thyself and us. Yet through all the misunderstandings his inner intent held true. Jesus' aim, and his achievement, was a double identification, one that linked him to, and made him, both God and man.

First of all was his identification of himself with God, as Son with Father. This was clearly an identification of Type 2, the identification of devotion, of worship. His first recorded words indicate which way the wind of the Spirit was blowing in his mind. "I must be in my Father's house" or "about my Father's business." Here is an identification, no doubt incomplete, yet true, as a twelve-year-old child's insights may be indelibly true, of his own interests with the interests of God. This, we know, went on all his life to the very end. It was the decisive, central factor in his character. It motivated his prayers, it directed his steps, it governed his choice of friends. ("Whoever does the will of God is my brother, and sister, and mother.") It was the inspiration of his life's driving interest in the Kingdom of God. It came to a climax in Gethsemane, in the prayer, "Not my will, but thine, be done." And it is heard in his last prayer of all, "Father, into thy hands I commit my spirit!" The fourth evangelist, the biographer of Jesus who lays most stress on Jesus' supernatural origin and power, the one who reports Jesus most often as emphasizing his filial relation to God, nevertheless testifies to the reverence and complete devotion of Jesus' mind. Even after the resurrection Jesus is reported as saying, ". . . my Father and your Father . . . my God and your God." There is no familiarity, no arrogance; the humility and the devotion are still there. Indeed, the choice of the word "Father" for God is itself an indication of Jesus' attitude of identification. No other word of all that were available for him out of the wealth of his religious tradition

could so well have made clear his active and continuous conception of the pattern of his own life as one lived by the pattern of
God. He does more than merely accept the divine will; he so to
speak throws himself into it, he seeks it. It is his food and drink;
it is what keeps him on his course, what gives meaning to life
itself and casts a gleam even through the shadows of death.

But this did not shut him off from common men, in contrast
with some would-be saints. Varied types of men, time out of
mind, have shown a single-minded devotion to God, or what
they thought was God. Why do we acknowledge some as saints
but to others allow no better name than fanatic? Saint and fanatic
are both devoted, both exert the identification of devotion, both
are selfless—but no, that is the mistake. They are both selfless
only in the sense that their personal desire is to be absorbed in
the will and purpose of God. But the fanatic has no mind or heart
left for others. For him, in all the world there are only two persons who count: God, and himself because he has thrown himself
and his destiny in with God. But the saint, though wholly devoted
to God, has a heart set free for devotion to God's creatures.
The fanatic overlooks Jesus; the saint takes Jesus in this as in all
things for his guide.

This brings us to the other basic identification of Christ: his
identification with men. All high men undergo the temptation
to cut loose from the masses of men who live, think, enjoy, and
hope on a low plane. "He travels the fastest who travels alone"
is a proverb held to apply to the aspirant for heavenly honors
not less than for this world's rewards. Now Jesus, if for no other
reason than the high quality of his humanity, was cut off from
men in various ways. His best friends continually misunderstood
him; two of them he called devils to their faces. His final rejection was by the "best" men of his time. Nevertheless, while
Jesus was tragically cut off, he never cut himself off. On the contrary, he was always trying to break through to the dull and the
disinclined.

The matter goes deeper than the efforts of a sensitive and
devoted man to stimulate others to a like spiritual insight and

devotion. Christ was more than a healthy physician giving medicines and advice to sickly people. He was trying to get through to people with whom he identified *himself*. This would be amazing, if we were hearing it for the first time. That one devoted to God should take pity on the unfortunates of the earth, this had been heard of before; but that one who so identified himself with God as Jesus did, could even *wish* to identify himself with man, this would seem to be madness. There is, I admit, a kind of paradox here; for Jesus both did, and did not, identify himself with men selectively. He said, "Whoever does the will of God is my brother, and sister, and mother" (Mark 3:35). If this means anything it means that he was fully aware that his relations with some persons could be closer than his relations with most persons. He journeyed by the narrow way; and those who found that road, he said, were few. Nevertheless, the other side of the paradox is that he does identify himself with acknowledged sinners.

Here the Atonement begins to take unmistakable shape. For the point and the problem of all religions is: How can man come to terms with God? For Christians the problem is especially poignant, for we recognize the reality and the gravity of sin as few if any other religions do, and we hold, not arbitrarily nor proudly, but because God has graciously shown us—we hold an exalted view of God. The God we know will not condone sin— he does not play with death so. And we have already questioned whether he can indulge in the monstrous make-believe of pretending the past was not the past.

If the Christian religion is different from other religions, radically so, it is not that its deepest question is different. It is the same cry in all religions: What shall I do to be saved? Christianity differs in its answer, not in its question. One strand in our answer is that the question is badly put. We hear in the New Testament of a man who asked that question, and we all know the reply: Believe on the Lord Jesus Christ and you will be saved. But reading on, we find that Paul did not give the man a lecture on the nature of belief. He talked to him about Jesus. The

Christian, answering the question, What must I do to be saved? begins by saying: What you need to ask is rather: What has God done to save me? Will he do anything to save me? Well, he *has* done it; what you need at the very first is not to do but to be done to. A drowning man does not need to manufacture a life preserver, much less to invent it. What he needs to do is to seize it. Salvation, the beginning of it, is not doing some great thing that will make God proud of us. Salvation begins by letting the stream of God's healing flow over us.

It would be absurd for me to survey the whole doctrine of the Atonement in a few pages. But I submit two well-worn presuppositions at this point, and venture three propositions. The first presupposition is that the life and death of Christ cannot be separated in any right doctrine of the Atonement. Protestant scholasticism, although it has legalized and formalized the work of Christ in a way that would scandalize the writers of the New Testament, nevertheless deserves the credit for emphasizing always this indispensable connection between Christ's life and death. Christ came into the world to be and to do, not simply to suffer and to perish.[4] The second presupposition is this: that our church's theory of the Atonement is basically true as far as it goes, and may well serve as the base line for other theories of the Atonement, all of which together are needed for a right understanding of what Christ means. Our belief is that what Christ did was to bring God and man together—that is, to actualize the identification-of-love initiated by the Father, of which something has already been said; and that the rationale of this was a vicarious self-giving on man's behalf and in man's stead—in short, what is often written off without examination, a "substitutionary" theory of the Atonement, if we may speak of an explanation or theory about what should awe rather than intrigue us. The presupposition, I repeat, is that the theory is basically true.[5]

Presupposing this, our three propositions are these: (1) **The doctrine of the Atonement is better expressed in terms of identification than in the legal terms with which Protestant orthodoxy** has been too well content. To put it another way: The principle of identification throws light, *from within,* on the doctrine of substitution. Without this illumination, the doctrine is a dark shell, a severely simple logical structure with no light or warmth. Without the principle of identification, the Atonement looks like a purely legal transaction along lines guaranteed to be legal by Turretin, Louis Berkhof, and who knows what other experts.[6]

As has often been remarked (e.g., by Robert Paul), "The most damning criticism of the penal [substitutionary] theory has always been that it is fundamentally unjust to transfer punishment from those who are guilty to One who is innocent."[7] James Denney, defender of a substitutionary doctrine, repudiates the forensic form of it. "There is nothing that I should wish to reprobate more whole-heartedly than the conception which is expressed by these words [forensic, legal, judicial]. To say that the relations of God and man are forensic is to say that they are regulated by statute—that sin is a breach of statute—that the sinner is a criminal—and that God adjudicates on him by interpreting the statute in its application to his case. Everybody knows that that is a travesty of the truth."[8] With the principle of identification, on the other hand, the doctrine of vicarious or substitutionary Atonement is felt to have both light and power. I am only trying to say explicitly what seems always to have been implicit in it, what the New Testament strongly suggests, what various writers on the Atonement have pointed out,[9] and what many a Christian has felt deep in his soul.

The second and third propositions should be stated side by side. (2) In all of Christ's living and dying, he identified himself with man in the way we have dryly called Type 2, the identification of devotion. He made himself one with man. (3) In all of Christ's living and dying, he aimed at identifying man with himself in the way we have called Type 3, the identification of drawing-in. This precisely mirrors God's identification-of-love with man and especially with his "people." As Christ lost himself in and for man, so his deep desire is that men may lose themselves in and for him, to the end that they may find life. The one type of identification is summed up in the few words, "The Son of man . . . came . . . to give his life . . ." (Mark 10:45). The other type (3) is expressed in the words, "I . . . will draw all men to myself" (John 12:32), or again, "Whoever loses his life for my sake, he will save it" (Luke 9:24). Both types come together in those words of prayer: "As thou, Father, art in me, and I in thee, that they also may be in us . . ." (John 17:21).

We said that Christ identified himself with acknowledged sinners. Though this may strain our faith, his identification could have had no *saving* effect if he had not identified himself with those who needed salvation. Goethe, I think, identified himself with man, and so did Walt Whitman; but neither of them as Jesus did. Goethe identified himself with all that is best in man; he was a natural aristocrat. Walt Whitman was a natural democrat; he could have said with that ancient Roman, *"Nil humani a me alienum puto."* But that Roman, and our Whitman, were unlike Christ in their difference of purpose. There seems to be no moral end in Whitman's identification of himself with the throngs of a great city. It is imaginative, dramatic, poetic, what you will; but it is not redemptive. As for Goethe, he was neither redemptive nor understood redemption.

Contrast Jesus, who identified himself with weak men, men who sin, beaten men. This began, to the outward eye, at the Baptism; but who shall say that this occurred first to Jesus at that time? The church has long been embarrassed by this story. We have days to celebrate all other outstanding events in the life of Christ, but none for the Baptism. What embarrasses the church is that baptism, especially and explicitly that of John, symbolizes repentance, confession, the washing away of sins. Some have thought that Jesus' reason for seeking baptism was quite different from that of anyone else: for others it was an actual declaration of repentance, but for him a purely formal requirement which he recognized and punctiliously fulfilled, *pro forma*. This explanation reduces the Baptism to something like etiquette, or a mere formal compliance with an ordinance. Besides, baptism was in no sense a clear requirement of the Mosaic Law. If it was a work of supererogation, then we are asserting it to have been a pure form, empty of meaning—and how could such a purely formal act indicate an extra degree of holiness? If, however, it was *not* a work of supererogation, it is difficult to see what meaning it could have had if it did not have the meaning attributed to it by John the Baptist and by everyone else. In either case, it is strange that Jesus, who everywhere else sought for meaning rather than form, and who indeed hated formalism, could have submitted to a rite which for him, on this theory, could have been no better than a formality.

Others, at the opposite extreme, have found in the Baptism an indication that Jesus felt himself to be a sinner, and thus openly expressed repentance for his sins. For those who believe in the personal sinlessness of Jesus, as I do, this is an impossible view. It is a fact, as Rafael Sabatini pointed out in his *Life of Christ,* that in all Jesus' life he never, so far as we know, gave any sign of a remembered conversion. No memory of past sins haunted him as it did Paul and Augustine and many another saint. The more saintly the soul, the more he mourns his early wilderness wanderings. But Jesus never suggests that he was at any time turned back from the road to destruction. As little did he express any gratitude for sins forgiven. He lived a life of gratitude; but not the gratitude of one who, having been much forgiven, loves much.

I submit that the Baptism was the open, public, dramatic avowal by Jesus of what may have lain in his mind for a long time, or may have suddenly emerged into consciousness that morning by the Jordan: namely, his identification with sinners. John's preaching, his baptizing, his demand for decision, split that crowd into two parts. There were those who confessed their sins in baptism; there were those also who stood aloof, admitting nothing. They were in fact all sinners; Jesus knew that. But he set himself in the place of those who acknowledged themselves for what they were. If he must take sides (and I do not mean that he was pushed into this), he had no hesitation. He made himself, then and thenceforward, one with the sinful human race. The

Pharisees by their attitude implied either that they repudiated the human race, or that they alone were human, while the *canaille* seeking baptism were something that had forfeited humanity. Jesus Christ would not repudiate the human race; he would not identify himself with what was inhuman. When does a man achieve humanity? The prodigal son comes to himself at the moment of starting home. Repentance is not to be beside oneself, it is to come to oneself.

Which is the more fully human, a Goethe who scarcely feels a sense of sin, or a Luther who goes through life with strong crying and tears? Jesus did not claim exemption. Knowing himself to be human, pressing into humanity, feeling the weight of human sin, baptism for him was natural and right. Jesus knew no sin by inner defilement. He knew no sin by personal participation and consent. Whatever bitter memories he may have acquired, sins of his own were no part of these. Nevertheless he did know sin as we do not. He knew sin by being "made to be sin" . . . But that did not happen first at Calvary. It is not simply that at the end of life, as an afterthought or as an end long awaited, Jesus at last identified himself with sinners for a few anguished hours. From beginning to end he was burdened with it. Here speaks the truth of what is called vicarious repentance.[10] Sin would have been no burden had he not identified himself with those who sin. All his life from this event right on to the end, where he prayed for those who were murdering him, it was so obvious where his identification pointed that he was called the friend of sinners, even himself a sinner. I say this did not begin at Calvary; it could already be seen on the day when Jesus made the sign of contrition and confession marking him brother to mankind.

There is no need of going through the life of Jesus to see how this worked out. If Jesus were going to identify himself with humanity it must be at the lowest level. The temptations in the wilderness, whatever else they mean, have this in common, that they invited Jesus to identify himself with humanity's topmost level. This he steadily resisted. In his unique picture of the Last

Judgment, the Son of Man identifies himself with the least and
lowest; yet not as if he were selecting one single layer of mankind
as the layer where he belongs. That would be a sort of reverse
pride. Rather, this *is* mankind, this sorry procession of the poor,
the needy, the beaten. Jesus' admirers have usually associated
him with royalty and with priesthood. But not so Jesus of
Nazareth. He made himself one with the many, the masses.

Then was Christ a class-savior after all? Is it suggested that
his identification after all was not with the world but with the
proletariat? By no means. None knew better than he that the
high and the mighty may well have tattered souls; that a man
may dine sumptuously every day, yet inwardly scrounge for
husks. It is with broken men that Jesus identified himself, broken
without or within. And *broken man* is only another way of saying
man.

So, what were Gethsemane and Calvary? That Jesus bore our
sorrows, that he carried our sins in his own body up to the Tree,
was no afterthought of a church grown more generous than he. It
was in Jesus' own mind, it weighed upon him, it all but crushed
him. Now the Suffering Servant ceases to be a role or an image,
and reaches its most acute reality. When Calvary's hour came,
it was not as if Christ had been waiting in some anteroom of
destiny for his hour to strike. If he bore our sins on Calvary, it
was the last mile of a long, long journey.

Yet it was a journey of devoted love. Herein lies the profound
difference between imputation in the sense criticized in the third
chapter, and the imputation of our sins to Christ. Protestant
scholasticism wants to have "symmetry" here; it is one of the
professed motives for erecting the classical theory of imputation
of Adam's sin. Yet one can scarcely imagine anything less symmetrical than these two imputations—that of Adam's sin to us,
and that of our sins to Christ. The one is a pure legal fiction,
based on no real agreement. The other is a real act of pure love.
"The LORD has laid on him the iniquity of us all," it is written;
but without the consent freely given, without the initiative of
Christ, without that lifelong identification of himself with us all,

God's laying our sins to his charge would have been just another legal fiction, an identification unjustified because invalid. Further, while the supposed imputation of Adam's sin, even if true, would be unjustified because of its enormous enhancement of evil, on the contrary the imputation of our sins to Christ is justified (if for no other reason) because of its incalculable enhancement of good. And how is it that Christ *could* be our substitute? Not by virtue of a transaction of some legal nature, not in fulfillment of a contract, not by court appointment. He could be our Substitute for the reason that not only then and there on Good Friday, but as far back as we can trace the current of his mind, he *willed* to be one with every man.[11] So taking our place, he suffered our fate. Far more than our fate, indeed; for he was aware, as we are not, of the depth of the sin, the width of the estrangement, dividing heavenly Father from earthly children.

The old orthodox teaching is simple: Christ as our substitute suffered the displeasure of God in our place; we then in his place enjoy the liberating "Not Guilty" from the judgment throne of God. In terms of the courtroom alone, that is a perpetration of ghastly injustice at worst, an arbitrary courtroom procedure at best. Seen in the light of the double self-identification of Christ —with God, with man—it is still a mystery, but it glows with light. This is not yet atonement; that depends on further identification, as we shall see. This is justification, without which there is no atonement. This is the groundwork, this the necessary foundation; this is God's part.

For in all this we have to remember that third kind of identification—the drawing-in kind, we have called it. All that Christ did and suffered on the cross and throughout his life would be pointless self-sacrifice; it would be like a mountain climber leaping ropeless and hopeless from a thousand-foot cliff for the sake of a comrade already smashed by his own fall . . . unless there were also the aim and intent of Christ, not merely that he should penetrate the life of man down to the roots, the rotten roots, but that he should draw the life of man up into his own. That the Highest shares the fate of the lowest is feck-

less and a great waste, unless there be also the will and intent—
and the power as well—to raise the lowest to the life of the
Highest. So we dare to believe that in Christ's own intention,
an intention fully transparent to the mind of God, both these
identifications blend, the devoting and the drawing: so to identify himself with men that when God looks at men he shall
see Christ, and when he looks at Christ he sees mankind.

But is this true or make-believe? Are all of these interlinked
identifications valid and justified? These questions must be postponed for the moment. For meanwhile there is another self-
identification of Christ which calls for our attention.

The Risen Christ: The Church

Something must be said now about what may
be considered even more speculative than what has gone before:
the identification, or identifications, of the *risen Christ*. It is not
possible to think of the relation of the risen Christ to individual
Christians apart from their relation to him; this will fall to be
discussed in our next chapter. However, something must be said
here, even if no more than by way of asking questions, about the
relation of the risen Christ, now, to the church of today. We are
thinking about the visible church; but let it be granted that we
have the privilege of speculating, as the church does, beyond
our line of sight, provided we do not take our thoughts for
God's blueprints.

First of all, what do we mean by the "risen Christ"? At least,
we mean Christ as he is and has been since the Ascension. We
reject the notion of Christ as a bare symbol or picture, in favor
of the New Testament conviction that he "ever liveth." Merely
to say this much raises unanswerable questions. The church herself is quite vague about what she declares so positively. Is Christ
in the same state that all saints enjoy, or is he existent in some
special form of his own? Is there anything physical about him?
Wherein does his human nature now consist? The assumption
made here, for purpose of very brief discussion, is that Christ

does exist (whether as Jesus Christ or not is a problem); that he is not less truly God and truly man than he ever was; but that his mode of existence, of presence, and of action, is much more like that of the Spirit (of whom more later) than like that of the man Jesus of Nazareth; that he is aware, has intentions, yes, even joys and sorrows; that he has not abandoned the identifications of which we have so inadequately spoken, nor repudiated their effects. In short, to use simple language, he has not given up his interest in this world; but on the contrary, this world is the scene of his central concern.

Here, because it casts light on a contemporary question, we may note a point at which our church, at any rate, makes the problem of the risen Christ even more difficult. We affirm that Christ remains both divine and human *forever*. The identification of God and man in the Incarnation, in other words, is not temporary but permanent, indeed eternal. The profound problem this raises with respect to the being of the Trinity we leave unexplored, not only because of its baffling nature but because it is not on our line.

There is another question often asked in our space-conscious era: If there are other races in other galaxies, should we preach the gospel to them? To put the same question another way: If there are such races in far places of the universe, does Christ have anything to do with them? If we accept the church's doctrine that Christ's humanity is indelible and eternal, the correct answer is, I think, something like this: Either those supposed races are human or they are not. If they are human, as human as we are, then we have no right to assume that Christ willed an identification exclusively with human beings on this planet, any more than that he willed an identification exclusively with the men living in the first century or in western Asia. Temporal or geographical limitation of the reference and relevance of the Incarnation has always been considered unthinkable. Whether these hypothetical galactic cousins of ours are *sinners* is another question. If so, they need the gospel; and since the gospel is centered in this great identification, all human beings, whether living blocks from here or light-millenniums away across space, need it and can be saved by it. But even if not sinners, if human they still need Christ; and it is not inconceivable that the risen Christ makes contacts of which we know nothing. If, on the other hand, those other races, assumed to exist, are not human, then we have no reason whatever to suppose that Christ is identified with them as with us. At least we should have to revise our creed and say that Christ exists, not "in two distinct natures, and one person"[12] but "in who knows how many natures forever." That God is manifest in many ways we believe; but his manifestations to non-human people are no more our affair than the religion of crocodiles. Christ's concern, now and forever, is with *man*.[13]

Coming now back home to more answerable questions: Already we have declined to sign the proposition that the church is the extension of the Incarnation. That proposition seems to arise from a notion of identity, which can be shown not to exist. There is room, however, for a theory of identification, which is another matter. Granted that a group of persons, as a group, is an entity which is other than the simple sum of its members, there is nothing too forbidding in the notion that Christ can have a direct relation to the church collectively as well as to Christians individually. This is *not* saying that there is such a thing as a "church" above, beyond, different from, or holier than its members. The church is always concrete, always personal, because it always consists of persons. Now the relation of Christ to the church which is in focus at the moment, is to the church as a whole, not to individuals as such; that will be taken up later. If we can go so far as to say there is an identification here, are we not led again to the proposition, the church is divine? And does that not remove the objection to thinking it the extension of the Incarnation?

We could settle this question shortly by simply pointing out that in the New Testament, even those who are most intimately related to Christ are never thereby elevated to the level of deity; and that therefore no identification of Christ with the church can properly be a basis for a claim that the church is divine or even sinless.

But we may further ask: What kind of identification is this between the risen Christ and the church as such? It cannot be the first type, for no one can be the detached, disinterested observer. It cannot be the fourth or fifth varieties, because each of these involves an identity, and we have seen reasons for denying that the church simply *is* Christ, or vice versa.[14] The kind of identification might logically be the second or third, just as we say was the case with identification between Christ and man.

Now the relation of God with persons, or indeed any relation where persons are concerned, is not likely to be a fixed thing. There is history in it; *what* it is depends on *when* it is. So, the case is different now from what it was, let us say, in the time of the historic Jesus and long before. Then, there was no Christian church; no one had believed Jesus or believed in him. The forces set in motion on Easter and at Pentecost had not yet very perceptibly stirred. Now, there are nineteen centuries of Christian experience, service, fellowship, and sins on the record. What is *now* the identification of Christ with the collectivity, the mixture of his people and no-people, called the visible church?

Let us venture a reasonable surmise: If the identification which Jesus willed and cherished throughout his adult life was the identification of devotion (our Type 2), *in order to the realization of the other kind willed at the same time* (our Type 3), the stress then must have been on the identification of devotion. The devotion was a fact, a blood-red fact. The response was in the future, it was something for which Jesus still prayed. Now, the devotion is in one sense a finished fact. Christ has no call to another crucifixion. His sacrifice was made once for all. Now, the response is coming, it is here, it has been operating through these 1900 years.

So—it is not rash to suggest that vis-à-vis the church and Christ, this is the era of the identification we called Type 3, the one in which the identifier makes the identified a part of himself, including within his own self, *without destroying them*,[15] the beings of those on whom he sets his love. This is the era of the identification of love, or rather the era when the identification of love is at work, successfully, with power. If this is the case, then divinity is ruled out for the church quite as much as for individuals. In those kinds of identification which do not begin with identity—and this one does not—what is "other" remains so. The peculiar feature of identification is that it deals with two entities, who do not cease to be two. If the identification be between the human and the divine, the human remains human, the divine divine. The more Christ draws into himself a person or a church, the more the humanity of that person and that church is enhanced, not blurred or diminished.

All this may cast a little light on the situation of the church today or any day. Christians themselves, who love the church and owe their very life, spiritually speaking, to it or to her, who indeed never knew Christ apart from the church, I say Christians themselves become discouraged about the church. It is not what it should be, indeed it is most things it should not be. It is of no use to withdraw, with other like-minded souls, to form a purer fellowship. That has been tried, and the results are not happy ones. It is of no use to try to reform the church (we think in our discouraged moments)—look at the devoted men and women who have spent their lives in vain, trying to do just that. It is of no comfort to point away to the Invisible Church, for it is not only composed of sinners, like the visible church, but its members do not recognize one another with certainty—who knows who belongs? These and many other questions dog the Christian who wants to believe in the church as his holy Mother and would do so except that her weekly binges discourage him.

The clue to hope here is in that special kind of identification which we have fixed on as *the* characteristic type activated by the risen Christ—the in-drawing, transforming kind. There is a point about it which we have not noticed until now: unlike the other types, this one is gradual. The other identifications may be, and some are inevitably, instantaneous. This one is seldom instantaneous, and perhaps in this world is never complete. So the church of Christ, which he is to present before God without spot or wrinkle, is not yet capable of filling that description. She is the church on the way, the church in process, the church immature; but Christ's church nonetheless. We see not yet all things beneath the feet of Jesus; yet we hail him Lord of lords. If the clue to the Christian life is growth toward and not in glory, why not the growth of the church in the same way? The goal of perfection in Christ—and this does not mean deity—is hers, and it is sure. But there is no way of reaching perfection except through imperfection. This is not to say that sin is not sin but only a phase of growth. It *is* to say that we have good reason to look forward to the day when Christ's intention in his every identification will be fulfilled.

6. I The *Identifications* of a Christian

There are two ways for sunlight to illuminate a stained-glass window. One is observed by a man standing outside the church in the street. The other is observed by a man standing inside the church. Same window, same sunlight. The difference is where the observer stands. So, the illumination which is available in this principle of identification brings out the design and the beauty of the Christian life only for those who stand within it.

Further, it must be remembered that identification involves two persons, not one alone; and cannot be passive, for it is always an act, a process. In an identity nothing new happens, it is just there. In an identification, something does happen, something is there which was not there before.

We shall have occasion to see how in every part of the Christian life, doctrines and truths which otherwise are correctly placed but dull, like that window seen from the outside, come alight with beauty when illumined by this pervasive spiritual principle. I say it is spiritual and not only logical, for it has most intimately to do with the things of the spirit. Most readers could complete this last chapter unassisted; once the idea has been accepted, illustrations from life will occur in profusion to any Christian who sits down to think about it.

The Atonement

First of all, the Atonement. If the meaning of life cannot be found by man apart from his relation to God, if the destiny of man is to glorify and enjoy God forever, and if the basic trouble with man is precisely the breakdown and breaking off of this relation, then till harmony has been restored, till the broken and repudiated identification of man and his Maker—the image of God—has been brought to life again, there is no atonement. The standard etymology is at-one-ment—which is just what identification is.

The Atonement is usually presented as something done exclusively by God. Certainly what God has done is indispensable. It is both logically and chronologically prior to anything man does or thinks. Some of our forefathers, in their zeal to affirm that salvation is of God, exaggerated the case. They invented the metaphor (not Biblical) *"truncus et lapis"* (literally, a log and a rock) to describe the condition of unsaved man. They used the expression (Westminster Confession of Faith, Chapter XII, §II) "entirely passive"—an idea implicitly corrected in a more recent chapter (IX, §II). Exaggeration though this is, it is the exaggeration of a truth, namely, that if God leaves us alone we are without hope. It is an exaggeration also of another truth: that the Atonement is something provided and offered, not earned and merited. Further, the Atonement is as complete as it *can* be, when we first discover it. It is not as if we made out an application blank and God replied (pardon the flippant sound): Your application will be placed on file; we will see what we can do for you. On the contrary, what God can do has been done, and it is a miracle every step of the way.

When a man stumbles onto salvation, as in Jesus' parable of the treasure hid in the field, or finds it after long search, as in the story of the pearl of great price, three great identifications have already been made, and we have looked at them in turn. First the great Identification of the Incarnation, the coming of the

Word, God associating himself (our creed says, forever) with man. Then there are the two great identifications of Christ: with God and with man. Both, one may say, are identifications of devotion, yet they are contrasted. Christ's identification of himself with God is the identification of worship, but no one could accuse Jesus of worshiping at the shrine of humanity. He would not call any man good, much less adorable. His identification with God the Father was one of submission, obedience, subjection if you like. His identification with man meant devotion, but it was the devotion of a superior to an inferior, a mother to her children or the captain of a ship to his crew. Both these identifications were alike in that Jesus wanted to be counted: with God, and with man. His identification with man had two aspects: he willed to *be* man, and also to devote himself *to* man; to be *of* the human race and *for* the human race.

This devotion, this determination to take the form of a servant, was not an end in itself. He desired this, yes; but it was part of a double desire: to attend and to attract, to serve and to win. Greater love hath no man than this, that he lay down his life for his friends—that was the identification of devotion. If I be lifted up, I will draw all men unto me—that was the identification of attraction, of drawing-in. Now, on God's side, all barriers were down. There was nothing else that even God could do to restore the broken bond. Nothing else? One thing only: to force man's will, compel his assent, reconcile him against his will. One thing—but God would not do it. He would not treat man like a tree trunk or a rock. Not a single writer in the New Testament, not a converted person depicted on its pages, thinks of his conversion as of a tidal wave that washed him ashore without his choice or against his will. Paul, in whose case the hand of God was clearly in evidence, said years later to King Agrippa: "I was not disobedient to the heavenly vision." The vision was a bolt from the blue; it had the effect of an attack with a deadly weapon. Yet in retrospect, Paul can speak of it as something to which he could have been disobedient. Peter's sermon at Pentecost addresses persons whom he later

describes as "born anew" (1 Peter 1:3), but he does not address
them there in Jerusalem as logs and rocks. The very fact that
the Christians used the words *kerygma, kerusso, euangelion,* to
describe their missionary efforts, suggests that the news could
be understood, the heralding heeded. But it was more than an
announcement, it was a summons. "God . . . commands all men
everywhere to repent" (Acts 17:30). The good news was of something God had done, but the hearer was expected to say something besides Oh. God could have made himself irresistible; but
he did not. In the dry terms of our analysis, identification of the
first or second types can exist, after a fashion, without the will
or the knowledge of the identified; but identification of the
third type involves the consent, and more than the consent—the
active responding will and choice of the identified. If it be objected that this leaves too much to man's decision, we can only
say that to control man as one would a log or a rock is to treat
him as something less than a man, and this God does not do.
God deals personally with personal beings, as Dr. Oman laid it
out so beautifully years ago. Grace that left no option whatever
would not be grace, it would be something else. We should have
to say, By force were ye saved, and not of yourselves. Identity,
be it repeated, cannot result from an act of will. Identification
can and must. It may be achieved through suffering or gained
with magnificent ease; but it always comes to pass in living
persons.

We read in the Bible of devotion-identification which desired
the response of attraction-identification but did not get it. "I
spread out my hands all the day to a rebellious people," said
Isaiah (65:2). "I would . . . but ye would not," said Jesus
(see Matthew 23:37). "I would to God," Paul said to Agrippa,
"that not only you but also all who hear me this day might become such as I am" (Acts 26:29); but his wish did not come
true.

However, while on the one hand the desire of Christ to draw
all men unto him does not always meet response, response there
was, and somewhere always is. Response is not to be compelled,

but men do open the door, they do come to him. Theologians may argue over how it is done, philosophers may deny that it can be done, cynics may say it is never done; but it is done all the same.

I do not say that this responding is the prerequisite of atonement; it *is* the final moment, and the beginning moment, of the reconciliation. We do not have to become identified and then be rewarded by atonement. By the act of accepting Christ's identification, we are identified with him; that *is* the reconciliation.

But it is not completely simple after all. For salvation begins, on the Christian's part, with a threefold identification. First I accept the self-identification of Christ with man—including me —with all that it entails. I take him as one who has so identified himself with me, with all enmeshed humanity, that he is in very truth our substitute, both in his obedience and in his sacrifice. I accept this in humility and joy. But I accept also this other identification which our Lord willed: that is, our becoming one with him. Not for nothing does Paul speak of being crucified with Christ, dying with him, being buried with him. Each of us becomes like Barabbas of the legend, released for some reason he did not understand, stumbling out into empty streets, wandering till he comes upon the crosses whereon hang two of his friends and one man he does not know—falling down and crying out, That is my cross! That is where I belong!

And then I make the third identification, which is implied in the second and may be part of it: my personal identification of devotion to Christ, the identification of worship. It breathes in many songs; but unless it breathes in the heart, the songs have a brassy sound.

Why is it that sometimes men are found who can concur in all the major dogmas of Christianity, including the most orthodox affirmations about the person and work of Christ, and still miss the mark of true faith? It is because there is no identification. Mental assent is not identification. Assent may or may not be existential, identification *must* be. Similarly, refusal of mental assent may make some difference, or none. But refusal of identification is fatal, for it leaves me still a stranger to God. Propositions about Hamlet, for example, I can take or leave. But propositions about God call for response. If I say I don't care for Hamlet, that proves me a dullard at the worst. If I say I don't care for God, that is self-chosen damnation. You can take Hamlet or leave him. Hamlet doesn't care and you don't. But you cannot take God or leave him. God does care, and you will. To refuse the identifications of Christ—of God in Christ—is to invite the darkness.

Faith, Repentance, Forgiveness

Where is faith in all this? Just as we said that the completion of the circuit by man's acceptance and responsive identification is atonement—the contact, the union, the reconciliation which atonement is—so the acceptance and the commitment are acts of faith. Yet faith is not an act, that is to say not an act like other acts, not even a simple thing to do which God accepts in lieu of more elaborate requirements. Faith is an attitude, an atmosphere, a climate of the spirit, in which identification may be perceived, accepted, returned. An illustration I have myself used is, I now believe, wrong. A man is drowning and a sailor from a boat tosses him a life preserver. The drowning man seizes it and is pulled to safety. Taking hold of the life preserver, I said, was faith. But I should prefer to say now that faith is not even that much of an act. It is rather the turn of the mind to acceptance, the state of the whole disposition that prompts him to seize and not to push away. So faith in the Christian sense is the total disposition or set of mind and soul, out of which the identifications and acceptances arise.

A similar question is: Where does repentance come in? Instructed Christians are aware that the common English usage of the word "repent" is misleading. In Biblical use, especially in the New Testament, it does not, of course, mean merely to be sorry for something done or said, not even sorry enough to quit. Repent, in Greek, means to change the mind, not in the sense of revising an opinion about this or that, but a fundamental making-over of the mind. Repentance turns out to be a lifetime business; it comes at the opening of the Christian life and never wholly ceases. I would say that as faith is the prerequisite of identification, so repentance is *concomitant* with identification. A common example may be shown by a long-married husband and wife. Their oneness is far closer to completion when they have been married twenty-five years than when they were married only five. They are more fully identified with each other. At the same time, the way each one looks on life has been affected, perhaps unconsciously, by this growing identification. Where once there were sharp clashes, now there is deep agreement. Identification, it should be remembered, is seldom instantaneous among men; it is normally a process. And the Christian whose identification with the Lord has been growing for years will, in the end, have a different outlook on life. In other words, repentance in the New Testament sense is a continuing process. The identification produces the repentance, and the repentance induces further identification. One might sum up this much of it by saying that without faith there will be no identification and without identification there can be no repentance.

Far more difficult questions center around forgiveness. Atonement has just been defined without mentioning forgiveness; is this scriptural and justifiable? Has the problem of make-believe been solved? Is there any connection between forgiveness and identification? Let us try, though with strong hesitation, to lump all answers together in one short constructive statement.

First, let it be repeated that God does not condone sin, for reasons already seen. Second, he does not *pretend* to forgive. If there is anything real about God's relation to us, it is this. Call it forgiveness, call it justification—they are at least alike in treating actual offenders as non-offenders—we should feel God guilty of a colossal mockery if it were all a kind of game.

Forgiveness comes before atonement.[1] It is not, strictly speaking, something atonement makes possible, but the other way around. Or if this seems to go too strongly against traditional formulations, it may at least be agreed that the intention to forgive is a part of the intention to reconcile; that the latter could not exist without the former. Forgiveness is the negative side of atonement. It is the erasure, the sweeping-away, of sins; it is a restoration of the possibility of being reunited. Atonement is that for which forgiveness takes place. It is the positive closing of the circuit, the first stage of a long union. Forgiveness is the medicine for the fever, atonement the beginning of returning health.

If forgiveness makes atonement possible, what makes forgiveness possible? We can and must say that God's love makes it possible; but who can explain the love of God? Yet we can see what that love does: it effects that very first of the central identifications, the decision of the eternal Christ, one with God, to become one with man, together with the human Christ's two commitments, identification with God and with man. Granted these all to be real and valid, where is sin? God in Christ has now so identified himself with men at lowest level that he becomes not only the bearer of all men, but of all sinners and all sins. He took them—the sins, when he took us—the sinners.[2]

We have assumed all along, and must insist here, that all these identifications are real. If God was not actually and truly one with man, if the Incarnation is only a symbol for the way we look at things, we are still in our sins.

The old objection that one man cannot carry the sins of another is fair: one man cannot, one man did not. It is only in the light of this dual identification of Christ with God and with man that we can speak of Christ's carrying the sins of men. But what became of the sins? The fact of them was not magically made a non-fact. Looked at in one way, the sins crushed Jesus, defeated him, broke his heart and killed him. Looked at in another way, he defeated them. We in him were slain at Calvary; but we in him rose at Easter. This is bold language, but the church has always used it.

It has been said too that when God looks at Christ he sees us; and when he looks at us he sees Christ. This can be true only as make-believe if there is no real identification. But assuming it is real, then God does not have to "see it that way." That is the way it is. Theologians have talked much of the "transfer" of our sins to Christ. I suggest the word "transfusion." A transfer is an external transaction, transfusion is a life-sharing act.[3] I do not fancy that I am making a mystery plain. I am concerned only to contend for the reality of these interlinked identifications.

For many sensitive Christian thinkers, the point that sticks in their mind about any substitutionary theory of the Atonement is the "transfer of guilt." This constitutes, for them, the most serious moral offense and the complete metaphysical and personal impossibility of that theory. It certainly cannot be said that the penal theory (as, for instance, R. L. Dabney or A. A. Hodge taught it) is today the standard theory of Protestant churches, not even that of the Presbyterian church. What has killed it off, for so many, is this dual objection: Transfer of penalty, though possible, is unjust, because transfer of guilt is simply impossible.[4] Now I do not hold a brief for transfer of guilt, especially as it seems to be more of a theological construct than the "plain teaching of Scripture" it is said to be. Still, it may be suggested that if this aspect of the doctrine is to be maintained, it can be justified only if the principle of identification is admitted to be central. Simple transfer of guilt, as if it were something which can be weighed or measured—transfer viewed as a legal or even arbitrary procedure,[5] something effected by fiat, even with the consent of Christ, a piece of celestial bookkeeping—this is surely no better than a theological artifact, devoid of truth or beauty. But if we think of Christ Jesus, very God of very God, entering deeply and willingly into the life of man, the Representative Man, the one who can stand for all whom God sees in him, then we can see not only how he might have felt the guilt of man's sin but how he *must* have felt it.[6] James Denney has put it very strongly indeed: "In Christ God somehow takes part with sinners against Himself."[7] God could lay upon him the iniquity of us all, because he took it upon himself. On our own plane we know something of what it means to share guilt. When a criminal is executed, do not

Christians feel the shame of their whole commonwealth, that all our wisdom and good will can devise no other way to deal with this wrongdoer than to kill him? It has long been observed that the innocent may feel shame for another's wrongdoing far more keenly than the habitual offender who eats, and wipes his lips, and says, "I have done no wrong" (Proverbs 30:20).

My point is that, viewed as a forensic transaction and no more, transfer of guilt does seem like the legal fiction to end all fictions. But—viewed from within the circle of identification, transfer of guilt seems to be not only natural but inevitable. This does not imply that we can rationalize the mystery; far from it. For the next question throws us back into our ignorance: Very well, if God somehow, by virtue of his identification with man, took our sins, with our guilt, into himself, then what became of them? At this point the sins vanish from our sight. God takes them and does not give them back. He who knew no sin was made to be sin, for us. Christ carried our sins in his own body up to the Tree. God, for Christ's sake, has forgiven you. Whatever else this means, we may be sure that forgiveness is no make-believe when God is the Forgiver.

Then how do *we* forgive sins? That is another story. I venture the thought here that strictly speaking, no man can in his own right forgive another. No man can bear another's sins as the incarnate God did the sins of mankind. If one person forgives another, it is only by way of Calvary, as both accept and identify themselves with the forgiveness of God. Forgiver and forgiven alike depend on *his* forgiving, because all-suffering, love.

Life in the Spirit: Sanctification

Identification, further, is the secret and the method of sanctification.[8] Three New Testament phrases furnish the theme for all the variations: *Christ in you, God in you, the Holy Spirit in you*. These are such amazing thoughts that few Christians believe them seriously. But this *is* sanctification, the spiritual core of the Christian's life and growth: the progressive identification of his own life with that of the risen Christ, the indwelling Spirit, the Father to whom Christ prays: ". . . even as thou, Father, art in me, and I in thee, that they also may be in us . . . I in them and thou in me" (John 17:21, 23).[9]

Our very confusions about all this point in the direction of the Triune God. This commingling of names and powers is not accidental; it goes back to Christ himself. The Spirit motivates and controls Christ. The Spirit comes to him just at the time when he implicitly identifies himself with sinners. The Spirit even drives Christ to his temptations. He ascribes his power to the Holy Spirit (Matthew 12:28). He assures his friends that he must go away so that the Spirit may come, the Spirit who will identify himself with Christ. Later on, Paul can speak of the Holy Spirit in you, or Christ in you, with little if any discernible difference in meaning. Paul can even say that the Lord (Jesus) *is* the Spirit (2 Corinthians 3:17). Paul did not mean to assert an identity, as a modern theologian does who proposes to discard the doctrine of the Trinity on the ground that it is difficult to name any duty or function of the Spirit which is not already within the scope of the activities of the Logos. Paul knew, however, that the Lord Jesus and the Spirit were not identical. He often exhorts his friends to be Christ-like, to imitate Christ; but he never challenges them to be more like the Spirit. The Spirit came upon Jesus, not the other way around. The usage of Paul points to the experience of the church. It is extremely difficult to distinguish an experience with the Holy Spirit from an experience with the risen Christ. Perhaps they are not different. In any case, both Scripture usage and the wide experience of Christians point to what has already been brought out, namely, the will-to-identification within the Trinity itself.

There have been theologians who seem to have felt that the Holy Spirit might be in some way offended if his prerogatives were not assigned him, or if he were not given due credit for the service he performs. Quite the contrary: the Persons of the Trinity have a strange will to self-effacement. The Father does not choose to be known except through a Son; the Son makes himself of no account, and appears in the guise of a servant, for the behoof of man; and the Spirit has no more sublime desire than to introduce Christ to men. So it is no wonder that Christians naturally and variously call their growing life a life in the Spirit, a life in Christ, or a life in God (Galatians 5:16; Ephesians 1; Colossians 3:3).

But to return to our survey: Sanctification, or the process through which the human person becomes more God-like, is by no means a single act completed in a moment of time. It has a beginning, but no end in this life. "We . . . are *being changed*," Paul writes, "into his likeness" (2 Corinthians 3:18). "You are in the Spirit, if the Spirit . . . *dwells* in you" (Romans 8:9). Such expressions denote continuance, progress.

It is therefore not surprising to discover that the Holy Spirit is referred to interchangeably with Father and Son, and that sometimes it is hard to distinguish between the Spirit of God and human spirits.[10] The living Spirit emboldened Paul to identify the life of faith with the life of the unseen Christ within him. "I live by faith," he says in the next breath after "Christ . . . lives in me" (Galatians 2:19-21). "We have the mind of Christ," he says, evidently associating other Christians with himself (1 Corinthians 2:16). In Acts 14:23 we find Paul and Barnabas appointing elders; in Acts 20:28 Paul tells other elders that the Holy Spirit had made them guardians of the flock. "The transcendent power belongs to God and not to us" (2 Corinthians 4:7), he says, though he himself exercised it.

First readers of Paul might suppose that he preached a gospel of pure passivity—"Let go and let God"—but those who know Paul better, or know the Christian life from within, know that sanctification is not a matter of acting like sidewalk superintendents while a building is under construction, doing nothing but standing with our eyes glued to a hole in the fence, watching God's machinery building more stately mansions for our souls. Paul can describe the Christian life in the most active way, as we know. "Let us *cleanse ourselves*," he says (2 Corinthians 7:1) "and *make holiness perfect*." Ephesians 4 and 5, mystical as these chapters are, also abound in imperatives. Immediately after praising God who is "able to do far more abundantly than all that we ask or think" (Ephesians 3:20), he goes into the imperative mood. "Lead a life worthy of the calling to which you have been called . . . put off your old nature . . . be renewed . . . put on the new nature . . . be imitators of God . . . walk in love" (Ephesians 4-5, *passim*). The same epistle that begins with God's election, the lavish riches of his grace, the immeasurable greatness of the power of God in us, ends with a command to *be strong* for the terrible battle in the evil day, when the Christian needs every bit of God's armor he can lay his hands on.

When Paul is describing his own life it is often in the most vigorous terms. When I fight, he says, I do not beat the air (1 Corinthians 9:26). At the close of his life he does not look back on it as a life of peace of mind. "I have fought the good fight," he says, "I have finished the race" (2 Timothy 4:7). Men have been called activists, they have been labeled semi-Pelagian, for less.

Here is a riddle. Who lives the Christian life, God or the Christian? Here is Donald Baillie's "paradox of grace."[11] In place of all the argument over synergism and monergism, we might well take all these and similar paired-off expressions throughout the New Testament as indicating how pervasively the principle of identification, as between God and his people, operates in actual living. Identification is never wholly actualized without mutual consent and mutual desire. It is clear from the New Testament that God does not sanctify those who are not willing to put in the best they have, as God has already put in the best *he* has. Without the mutual desire, identification is invalid. The authentic Christian life is initiated by God, and its completion is in his power and purpose; but it will not come to pass apart from effort and desire on the part of the one who is being saved.

Reasons have already been given for distinguishing the "life in the spirit" from mysticism.[12] Since some intransigently Reformed theologians have not hesitated to speak of the "Unio

Mystica," I would not quarrel over the use of the word. But I prefer not to use it, because it is ambiguous and has connotations I do not mean to suggest. One example will suggest the kind of thing the New Testament is driving at. Abbé Nédoncelle describes in these words the effect which Cardinal Newman had on his followers:

"Each one discovered in him his own idealised 'I.' He offered to them the intuition of what they wanted to be in their heart of hearts. . . . He carried in him an aspect of themselves which was more real than their daily 'I,' and from which so far they had lived apart. . . . And this identity did not keep their friend from being altogether different from them. . . . it would be a much too facile psychology to explain facts of this sort by 'imitation.' The community of consciousnesses does not consist only in a sort of admiration . . . Love is not an exhortation but a sudden and irresistible complicity."[13] Jarrett-Kerr comments, "If this can be so even within the natural order of human relationships, how much more so will it be of man's relation to the Redeemer"—and, I would add, to God!

Walking by the Spirit: Ethics

After all this, we might expect to find identification operative in daily practice at all levels of the Christian life. We are not surprised, of course, to see persons with no claim to being Christian, living seclusive, self-seeking lives, repudiating anything like identification with God or man. The Germans had an expressive slang phrase which puts the whole attitude into three syllables: *Ohne mich!* Include me out, I don't want to get involved. Don't give your heart to a dog to tear, said Kipling. *A fortiori*, don't give your heart to a person to tear. This is sometimes known as the Harvard attitude; but there is no reason why Harvard should be saddled with it. There are those who hold this view of life who could not be admitted to Siwash, let alone Harvard. From this point of view, identification is not out of the picture entirely, but its place is altogether and selfishly instrumental. It is never seen as a good in itself, it is not used for good ends. For such persons it is a device, no more, for enhancing one's own ego.

This is not surprising. What is surprising is that many alleged Christians who, one would suppose, are committed to a life of identification along the lines we have sketched, at crucial moments in their practical affairs show plainly that they share the non-Christian view and not the Christian view of life. Why is this? Three reasons may be suggested. One may be that while they have heard about life in the Spirit, such as we were ideally describing just now, they regard this as something "out of this world," something only for postgraduate Christians. They forget that ever since Paul wrote of these matters to his substandard, low-income-bracket, underprivileged little congregations around the Aegean Sea, perhaps a majority of the Christians who have best demonstrated what life in the Spirit is have been plainest of the plain, neither religious geniuses nor any other kind. Another reason for the unwillingness of professed Christians to live a Christian ethical life, or even to inquire what it is, is the American fear of being impractical. Christianity is practical for preachers and invalids, but not for wage earners, moneymakers, conformists. A third reason for this depressing phenomenon may be that these persons are not yet actually *identified* Christians. Their identification with Christ, or with other persons, is verbal, such as it is; no more. If it is not too uncharitable a judgment, their actions or inactions raise the question, *Are* they Christians? Can a person who is a complete stranger to the experience and the attitude of identification, be counted truly a Christian? This is not a moralistic or legalistic judgment. This is not judging persons according as they don't do this or don't do that. It is rather the question whether, if the grapes do not appear in the cluster, this is a grapevine we have or a thornbush.

Identification with Christ and the Holy Spirit is an invisible thing. But where it exists visible results will ensue, and some of these will follow this pattern of identification in some of its forms. Let us look at one or two cases in point.

One is a much debated practical problem raised by John Calvin. It concerns the motive for a Christian's relation to others, especially when he tries to follow the directive, Let us do good to all men. Now Calvin believes that the image of God in men has never been totally destroyed. The worst of men is still a bearer of that image; the original intended identification of God with men has been broken and twisted, but though it is deface- able it is still indestructible. Calvin reminds his readers that the needy man, any man who needs your help, is, as the bearer of the image of God, God's "substitute." "The image of God, by which he is recommended to you, deserves your surrender of yourself and all that you possess." Calvin indeed doubts whether any other motive than this can induce us to love even those who hate us. "We must not reflect," he writes, "on the wickedness of men, but contemplate the Divine image in them; which, con- cealing and obliterating their faults, by its beauty and dignity allures us to embrace them in the arms of our love."[14] Here is a call for the Christianly inspired imagination. One might go a step beyond the writer to the Hebrews and say, Without imagi- nation it is not possible to love your fellow man nor to take him at his true value. To put this another way: for Calvin the love of neighbor is possible only when we think of the neighbor as identified with God. But how hard this is! Only the eye of in- spired imagination can read, beneath the scrawling lines of the palimpsest of an unworthy life, the veritable handwriting of God.

For many persons, perhaps for most, Calvin's thought here is too high and difficult. Very well, consider the one moral directive from the lips of Jesus which has been most widely ac- cepted, the Golden Rule. (Perhaps many think they accept it who do not, really, but let that pass.) Again we have a directive that calls for imaginative identification, this time not of God but of oneself with the neighbor. We shall not pursue this so-called rule into its practical puzzles and out again. It would delay us much too long. But we should find, if we did, that this too calls for a strong imagination, and that after all it is not a rule but a principle.

This leaves us, by the way, with another problem. If it turns out, after all, that the Golden Rule is not a rule, that we have to play the melody of life by ear, for lack of a printed score, then is life a long series of improvisations? Is there, after all, no foolproof set of rules that we can follow? One answer, often given, is that there are, to be sure, no foolproof rules—that rules of any sort have no place in the Christian life. I could not go along with this much of the answer, and I should not be orthodox if I did. But I must agree with the rest of it: namely, that what is desired, and what can be had, to guide the Christian on his way, is first of all not a rule nor a code but a Person. The Holy Spirit, we are told, is our faithful Guide, ever near the Christian's side. If what we were saying is true, that the Spirit is fully identified with God, and that it is possible and indeed normal for the Christian to become identified progressively with the divine Spirit, are not these identifications sufficient guarantee that one cannot go wrong? Is guidance by the Spirit a real thing or only a fancy? And if real, must it not carry infallibility with it? Fallible guidance would argue a fallible God.

This problem is pointed up by one of the great scandals of Christendom: that diametrically opposite or mutually exclusive views have been firmly, even violently, maintained by Christians who claimed with equal fervor and sincerity that they were speaking and acting under the guidance of the Holy Spirit. All we have to do is to remember the Reformation. When we were children, perhaps we grew up with the idea that the devoted Christians were all on one side—our side, of course. Then we learned that each side could claim its saintly men and women, martyrs and confessors. Jesus saw that such things were possible: "Whoever kills you will think he is offering service to God" (John 16:2). Now, when two conflicting certitudes meet head on, driven by conflicting convictions of what Christian loyalty calls for, only two conclusions are possible. Either one is right and the other wrong, or both can be wrong. Both cannot be right.

Facts like these, too abundant to be explained away, warn

us against the notion of infallibility, no matter how stubbornly maintained. Let us suppose for a moment that one is in error, while the other's claim to infallibility is justified. The problem then becomes, which is the infallible opinion? (We do not refer to problems of fact which can be settled by research and observation.) The decision may be made on the merits of the question, or on pragmatic grounds; but it cannot be settled on the basis of claims of infallible guidance alone, as the contestants would have us do.

We must be on the wrong track. Infallibility is *not* guaranteed. The Bible offers some examples of men who—we may believe—were really filled with the Spirit yet who made errors of fact or judgment. It was after Pentecost that Peter was still carrying out the old dietary laws, after Pentecost that he dissembled at Antioch and had to be called down by Paul. As for Paul, no one questions that he was a spiritual and Spirit-guided man; yet he himself admitted having said something he should not have said, at a meeting of the Sanhedrin. His quarrel with Barnabas over John Mark also comes to mind. Or one may recall any writer in the New Testament—and we call them all inspired, delicately sensitive to the Spirit of God, yet every one was mistaken about the time of the End. But why go back so far for illustrations? Many of us have known men who looked forward to the ministry with hope and faith . . . and then in time had to face the dismal fact: No one else, certainly no church, could believe that the pastorate was what God had in mind for them. Or consider those persons, known in every denomination, who felt the missionary call, were convinced that it was genuine— only to find out, suddenly or slowly, that it would be physically impossible for them to enter missionary service. It is rash to say that God calls people to do what his Providence puts out of the question.

So where are we? The conclusion is forced upon us that the presence of the Spirit is no guarantee of infallibility of observation, judgment, or expectation. Then what good does identification with the Spirit do anyone? Does the "spiritual man" have any advantage, when it comes to life's decisions, over the man of the world? What he does have, what he can absorb from contact with the divine Spirit, is the right *attitude,* the atmosphere in which decisions can be best made. God does not dictate to us what to think; if he did, we should be no better than machines chewing on the data that are fed them. Not what, but *how* to think, is the invaluable gift of the indwelling Spirit. "We have the mind of Christ" does not mean for Paul that what Christ knows, we know; it means that the motives that governed his thinking govern ours.

The Church:
The Community of Identification

We have been speaking of the Christian almost as if he were a lone adventurer in an unfriendly world. There is much truth in this. Yet it is not the whole story. For there exists what can be called the *Community of Identification,* wherein every encouragement is given to live the life of identification: namely, the church. Here we are embarrassed at the same time by the countless thousands of words that have been used, especially in recent years, to describe the church, and also by one's constant uncertainty how much of this is recognizable as a description of the church as it is. Furthermore, for all the flood of books and essays, the variance of opinions about the nature, marks, and limits of the church remains about as it was. Teaching ecclesiology is too much like delineating the bounds and the course of long-standing quarrels.

The motto, *Ubi Christus, ibi ecclesia,* is ambiguous. It is sound when it is used to distinguish between a formally correct church (i.e., with correct doctrine, correct exegesis, correct architecture, correct observance of the sacraments, correct law and discipline, but without any resemblance to Christ in spirit or practice) and a church (whether these matters be correct or not) which embodies and glorifies the *Agape* love which was

and is in Christ Jesus; between a church where Christ is defined
according to the latest interpretation of Chalcedon, and a
church where he is a living Presence. There are two things that
remind us of the dawn: an alarm clock, and roses in the garden.
There are two ways in which a church can remind the world of
Christ: by loud *kerygma* at 11:30 A.M. sharp every seventh day,
and by what Paul calls the odor of life unto life, all seven
days. It is this latter for which we should reserve the title
"church."

Yet this slogan, *Ubi Christus, ibi ecclesia,* can be misleading.
This would imply that if the human race were swept off this
planet, and Christ by his Spirit still be here, the church would
not cease to have existed. It would imply that a lone priest offering the Mass in an empty chapel could be the church. Rather,
as Brunner has urged, we should say, *Ubi koinonia, ibi ecclesia,*
the church is where the fellowship is. Or to put it in the terms
we have been using here: the church exists wherever there is an
actual, albeit imperfect, community of identification, in the
various Christian senses of that word.

Most of the names for the church in the New Testament suggest identification. It is called a brotherhood, a family.[15]

This raises a question, not out of our way. Is not the Christian family more truly a community of identification than the
church? We can say that it is generally more effective, not necessarily because it exemplifies more fully the principle of identification, but because the family lives in propinquity through the
week—or did in A.D. 50—and the church does not. But when the
church does operate as a community of identification, it is more
a triumph of grace than when a family so lives. A family is
bound together by natural ties, so much so that non-Christian
families sometimes have a more attractive and harmonious home
life than some which are composed of professed Christians. But
a church ideally is an *"omnium gatherum";* it may even be
called the fellowship of the uncongenial. That identification
should take place in the family is "only natural"; that it takes
place in the church is super-natural.

All the New Testament names for the church suggest identification. The most well-worn metaphor is that of the Body. This is not the place to argue whether this is the basic metaphor, but it certainly is appealing and revealing—a superb example of identification. The meaning of the body is given it by its tissues, and conversely the meaning of each tissue is to be learned only through its relation to, and function in, the whole.

The metaphor of the Bride is psychological, as that of the Body is physical. They both suggest unity in difference. As the body is not many but one, so the bride is one—single-minded, single-hearted. When the proposal of marriage was accepted she did not say, "Well, in some ways I suppose it is a good idea." When the important question is put to her at the ceremony, "Do you take this man . . . ?" she will not reply, "You know, I've half a mind to!" She may be, as most women are, of a plural nature; but her inner unity never was and never will be more complete and without reservation than it is on the day of her bridal. In yet another way this metaphor strongly suggests identification, for the bride is not only fully identified with her husband in her dominant heart's desire; she is entering a life where *without ceasing to be herself* she becomes a more complete self through being continually and progressively identified with the other.

So the dominant metaphors, what we may call the given names of the church, all suggest identification. The church is the only group life besides the family in which the principle of identification is explicit, and where reciprocally and mutually there is encouragement to its practice.

We have said that where there is no participation, there is no identification. On this score, it could too easily be said that the church itself belies what has just been said about it. What is it in which the church members participate? First of all, each one participates in the forgiveness of God. A recent radio speaker, however, attributed the low state of the church to the fact that the very notion of forgiveness has grown dim, and few among average church members, to say nothing of churchgoers, have actually experienced anything they could name as divine forgiveness. The speaker was probably right. For one thing, the average church member does not feel that God could have had much to forgive, in his case. For another, while the forgiveness and pardon of God are obliquely referred to in the questions asked him upon "joining the church" (pardon the language), the connection is only verbal. What the word "Savior" means, the church member seldom thinks. In short, while in theory the church is the fellowship of the forgiven, actually it is a collection of those who have been forgiven but don't know it.

Again, church members are sharers, by right, in a common hope. Ideally the church is the most optimistic body in the world. But is this true in fact? It does not appear so. Even when there is a sense of the future, there is disagreement as to what the future is. God is supposed to muddle through somehow, and meanwhile we give a passing occasional thought to the heaven we do not much believe in.

The Christian life has been called the life of gratitude, and so the church is ideally the fellowship of those who participate in a common gratitude. The epistles of the New Testament, show-ing what it was for which those early Christians (and not only the Apostles who preached to them) were grateful, do not have a modern sound. Ask the average church member to describe the difference between himself as he would be without God, and himself as he is with God. He will be hard put to it to give an intelligent answer. The difference between godless John Doe and godly John Doe (on John's own showing) is so slight that you wonder, and so does he, why we should send off missionaries thousands of miles to induce others to enjoy these microscopic changes.

Ideally also the members of the church participate in a com-mon devotion. It is true, they all repeat some of the same prayers in unison on Sundays. Forms of worship may be so standardized that no one can tell any more, without looking at the bulletin (and not always then), whether he is sitting in a Presbyterian, Episcopal, or Baptist church. But as for heartfelt devotion, it may be less unanimous than the unison prayers. The old hymn comes true, "Hosannas languish on our tongues, and our devotion dies."

So the church dwindles, and small wonder. It lacks the very feature which validates it and gives it a special and unique life. What should be a fellowship is not, for the identification which should be mutual and reciprocal is no more than proximity. A purpose which should set the heart afire is little understood; the central aim of the church is forgotten or disguised. Perhaps it was always thus. The church may be like the widow's jar of oil, always almost gone, never gone.

Nevertheless, there is always *something* which keeps the visible church going. There is something which, after all has been said, rewards those who diligently seek it. The church is not made up exclusively of average members, thank God. There are above-average members, and aside from churches which bear the specific name, there are fellowships without bounds or rules or names, the "two or three gathered together"; there are the cells of prayer, the emergency squads ready for service by day and night, there are the young people who are growing in grace and the knowledge of the Son of God. Indeed, if we could get rid of the habit of mistaking our church for *the* church, we might not be so discouraged. For all we do to prevent him, the Holy Spirit does come, and not all the churches to which he comes are in the telephone book. There *is* participation in forgiveness, in gratitude, in hope, and in devotion. Whatever be the outward form or no-form, the church is precisely the union of those in whom all the kinds of identification we have been trying to unravel unite.

We must be careful to keep in mind the sort of union this is expected to be. It is not like a reunion of a high school class, or a famous battalion, a collection of persons who have one set of memories more or less in common but who have no interest in one another aside from these. A church is not like a surgical ward where all the patients are sharing a present experience; not like a crowd on one side of a football stadium, their spirits going up and down together, but dispersing when the game is over, without so much as saying good-bye. These are temporary identifications, and uncreative. In a true church, wherein all are joined, severally and together, in fellowship with one another, with the church as an organism, and with the Holy Triunity, all of this works together to form a new entity, which is both corporate and personal. When Christians who are all and severally identified with Christ and with other Christians, come together —by way of worship or of service—power is released, not to destroy but to build. By force of their interresponsive givings and takings, their earnest desire to become one in Christ, they create what transcends the sum of their small selves, and they know what the words mean, Mother Church. No longer barren, such a church conceives and brings forth children by the power of the Holy Spirit.

And so, like all right identifications, this one also is justified by the fact that the sum total of good in the world is enhanced by the kind of unity the church is. Indeed Christ himself, so far as his triumphs in this world are concerned, amounts to more with the church than without it. If this were not so, he would not have chosen the Twelve. His parable of the Vine is much to the point here. The branch is nothing without the vine; but where is the vine apart from the branches? The cut-off branch withers; the cut-off stock is fruitless till new branches grow. Root and branch are the vine. The branch receives its life through the root; but the root creates its fruit through the branches. This may be what Ferré, and Augustine before him, mean by saying that Christ alone is not Christ; that Christians and the church are the whole Christ. Identification can go no further.

So at the high point of the church's worship are the sacraments, each of which in its own way is a symbol of identification. In Baptism the identification of this Christian with the Divine Fellowship is declared; by the Lord's Supper the identification is brought over and over to mind. The two sacraments support each other. As Baptism points to the irrevocable identification, the Eucharist points to the need for constant renewal. As bread and wine are shortly one with the body, so the Christian absorbs Christ into his inmost life.

And then what? That which is symbolized must be *lived*. At the first Communion in a small congregation, the minister had been conducting an evening service, where he spoke very earnestly; but his talk had been disturbed by the whispers of men in the corner who were thinking of something else. I know for a fact that of those who were there, only one man remembered the sermon. One of the little congregation got up and left in the middle of the service. It went beyond indifference and deafness of spirit. The minister knew that he was not carrying them with him. He was quite certain in his own mind that they were all pretty close to repudiating him altogether. It was only a matter of hours before they would be ready to accept his resignation. They took so little interest in his personal troubles—which were all but unbearable—that they could not stay awake long enough to know what they were. What would you have done? This Man prayed for them. "For their sake," he said, "I consecrate myself." They were not worth it, you would have said. They were not, indeed, but they were his own, and he loved them to the end. That is Identification.

> "The writ of loving well
> Still makes its old demands:
> A sometime residence in hell
> And nailprints in the hands."[16]

A Prayer

O God
O Light
O Strength
O Beauty supernal
Teach us to love Thee with all our minds.

The heaven of heavens cannot contain Thee,
    Still less can any definitions that we have built.
We send our slow trains of thought to reach Thee,
    We rise on wings of words into the blue incomprehensibles,
And all the time, Thou art nearer than breathing, closer than
      hands or feet.

Help us to find Thee not only in the star-flaming heavens
    But in the still small voice.

Undergird our certitudes,
Inspire our searchings,
Smite our self-assurance dumb.

In the name of the One whom to know is to live eternally,
    Jesus Christ our Lord.

Amen.

I *Appendix*

Not "the first that ever burst
Into that silent sea."

The best reason for this book is not that it marks an unprecedented discovery, as if the principle of identification had lain hidden and unknown all these centuries. A principle so pervasive in Scripture and experience (and we have been far from exhaustive in illustrations) can hardly have escaped the eye of theologians. While this may be the first book on the subject written in just this way, it is by no means the first notice that has been taken of this significant principle. For the benefit of readers who may wish to study the subject further, some writers of special interest in this connection will be mentioned here and their constructions very briefly compared with our own.

We should inquire, by the way, what the difference is, if any, between the principle of identification and the ancient orthodox doctrine of circumincession or perichoresis, and the kindred doctrine of *communicatio idiomatum*. The difference lies in the element of will and intent which, as envisaged here, constitutes the creative force of identification. They seem to be more akin or analogous to chemical phenomena than to personal activity. What is interchanged is attributes or qualities; the self is not *eo ipso* involved, as with identification.

The principle of identification has been recognized in Christian theology since earliest times, though not exclusively by professional theologians. Speaking for many psychologists, H. A. Overstreet (*About Ourselves*, W. W. Norton 1927, p. 44) writes that the one thing which deepens life, gives it resonance, and brings it joy is "putting oneself outside oneself into another personality." A precise description of identification, Type 2! As the indirect testimony of a novelist of theological leanings, Dostoevsky has Father Zossima saying (in *The Brothers Karamazov*): "Make yourself responsible for all men's sins. As soon as you sincerely make yourself responsible for all things and for all men, you will see at once that you have found salvation. . . ." (Book VI, ch. 3).

It would be valuable to pursue this principle through the thoughts of contemporary psychologists, novelists, and playwrights; but we are concerned with theologians. This is not a book about books, otherwise we should have begun in chapter 1 with the church Fathers, examined outstanding scholastics, and come on down into the present, not forgetting Schweitzer, Kagawa, and Gollwitzer. But in this appendix we note only a few of the thinkers who have taken special note of identification. St. Augustine's *Treatise on the Trinity* comes to mind. He was not satisfied with any of his analogies for the Trinity, but at any rate they all pointed in the same direction. The striving-for-unity in the Trinity of love is expressed in inadequate symbols, to be sure, but all point to identification. The Trinity, as Augustine conceives it, cannot be understood except in the framework of love.

Calvin is a fair example of the kinship between the Reformers and Augustine. In 1939 W. Kolfhaus came out with a thorough study of the Reformer's doctrine of union or communion with Christ (*Christusgemeinschaft bei Johannes Calvin*. Neukirchen, Kr. Moers 1939). Calvin makes much of this; but he is not a mystic in the way spoken of in our chapter 3. Union with Christ by faith is not the same as Christ-mysticism. Calvin uses many mystical expressions: union with Christ, being incorporated into him (or simply being in him), growing together with him into one body, mystical union, being made nothing, feeding on Christ. But he always links Christ and the Word, as mystics do not. He is cold to the possibility of new revelations, as mystics are not.

He is little inclined to the purely contemplative life. He was far
from being the kind of introvert that a typical mystic is. Visions
and ecstasies are made unnecessary by the union we have in
Christ. For Calvin, the basic relation of a man to God is that
of sinner to Judge; this is not the mystical view. For the mystic,
the Word of God is the finger pointing to the object, vanishing
once the object is seen; for Calvin, the Word is the light without
which not a step can be taken. For Calvin, there never is identity
between the worshiper and the Object of worship. Calvin could
express identification very strongly. We are members of the flesh
of Christ, "we coalesce, so to speak, into one life and substance,"
he says in a sermon on Galatians 3:26-29. But this is to be explained, Kolfhaus believes, by Calvin's explanation elsewhere,
that we are one with Christ not because he pours his substance
into us, but because by virtue of his spirit he shares with us his
life and whatever good he has received from the Father (p. 27).
As soon as we believe, we become members of him in truth, and
his life flows down to us. But one has to take such mystical expressions in the light of his general viewpoint; and this excludes
mysticism, though not the mystical. Calvin certainly had a more
vital notion of identification than some of his more legalistic
followers. He did not regard the act of justification as an isolated
one. Forgiveness of sins is not the cold sentence of a judge, but
an act springing from love, an act which sets us in community
(p. 62). Justification and ingrafting into Christ are not in the
relation of cause and effect, but denote one and the same act of
God (p. 60). Thus for Calvin justification was inseparable from
identification, on the one hand with Christ and on the other hand
with the Body of Christ, the Church.

One of the last of the nineteenth-century theologians was H. A.
Watson, whose book *The Incarnation and Personality* dates from
1920 (S.P.C.K.). He combines orthodoxy, as was perhaps typical
at that time, with the all-pervasive idealist philosophy. He believes
in a real incarnation, not a deified man but a humanized God;
but finds it hard to go all the way with the idea. He does, however, find the Incarnation, as the church does, unique. He teaches

a doctrine of identification without using the word; the Incarnation he describes as "the inclusion of humanity in deity and the bestowal of life, the divine gift, upon humanity" (p. 187). Yet this is not unique, after all. Those who allow themselves to express the best they feel within them may be said to practice the Incarnation. (This of course is to weaken the tragic element which a full identification would require.) "What Christ has done, man is now able to attempt to do" (p. 216). Inevitably this lowers the value of the Incarnation; if it is something we can try, ourselves, no wonder the author comes down to this: "Incarnation fosters in us the principle of self-respect. It encourages the principle of noblesse oblige, it stimulates us to rise to the occasion" (p. 201).

A Roman Catholic work of great learning and importance comes in the large twin volumes by Emile Mersch, S.J., a Belgian priest, both translated from the French: *The Whole Christ* (Bruce, Milwaukee, 1938) and *The Theology of the Mystical Body* (Herder, St. Louis and London, 1951). Mersch distinguishes two ways of conceiving the relation between Christ and the Christian: a reality of the moral order, and a "real and ontological union." He prefers the latter, though he recognizes the validity of the former. In the Church, the Body of Christ, there exists between the Incarnate One and each Christian a bond closer than resemblance, more than simple dependence, more than being a part of an organism, more than a bond of love. More than the closest moral union, it is a mystical, transcendent, supernatural union. The author accepts from Athanasius, and in fact emphasizes, the doctrine of divinization; there is no dividing line between the Word and the faithful. "In him the divinity deifies the human race" (*The Whole Christ,* pp. 584, 271). Though Mersch parodies Protestantism, he perhaps does not realize how much of what he says can be, and has been, said by Protestants. One peculiarly Roman Catholic notion which strikes the eye is the description of Mary as the "neck" (*sic*) through which all spiritual gifts are communicated to his mystical body (*op. cit.,* p. 568). However, Mersch has some profound expressions for what we have called identification. He calls it "this supernatural unity of mankind effected in the God-man . . . the perfecting [and, he adds, the divinization] of the unity effected in man" (*The Theology of the Mystical Body*, p. 128). "The Creator has become creature, the creature who is the Creator, by hypostatic union in Christ, by mystic union in Christians. This interchange, which is everything in Christianity, places man at the beginning and center of everything, because it places God in the heart of man" (*op. cit.*, p. 133). Refusal of unity (we should prefer, refusal of identification) is original sin (*op. cit.*, p. 146). This principle of interpenetration helps Mersch to understand how Christ can be Man by being a man. "All mankind is in every man," but now only in part. "Absolute human perfection . . . would require a man to be . . . interior to every man and that every man should be interior to him." Living his own life, he will at the same time share in all human life, experience all human suffering, and think all human thought. "This human universality should not in any way destroy man's inwardness, but should find complete expression by deeply participating in it without at the same time violating it by undergoing disintegration" (*op. cit.*, p. 118).

Of the theological constructions to which my own thoughts on identification are nearest, outstanding are those of the novelist-theologian Charles Williams and R. C. Moberly. (Williams, *The Descent of the Dove*; Oxford, New York, 1939, and also his novels. See also Mary McDermott Shideler's *The Theology of Romantic Love*—a study of Williams—Harper 1962.) Charles Williams had a strongly interpersonal doctrine of identification, for which his name was coinherence. Mutual or reciprocal identification is conveyed by this word; passages from John 17 are much to the point. Williams used freely also the terms substitution and exchange. "[Christ] by an act of substitution . . . restored substitution and co-inherence everywhere; up and down the ladder of that great substitution all our lesser substitutions run; within that sublime co-inherence all our lesser co-inherences inhere" (p. 235). The Trinity, he says further, "mutually co-inheres by Its own nature" (*ibid*). This idea, as Williams developed it, is obviously close to that developed in this book; but there are differences. For one thing, I can conceive of a one-sided identification, devotion which meets no appropriate response. Coinherence, however, appears to be mutual always. There is no Type 1 identification; indeed, coinherence appears to be only a reciprocal form of our Type 2. The question could be asked: Can there be abortive identification? Does or can identification exist when A is devoted to B but B rejects the devotion? Williams would perhaps say this is not coinherence; I should say that this is identification in fact, even if not reciprocal and possibly not complete. Williams has further a strong mystical tendency. He highlights a motto, source unknown: *This also is Thou; neither is this Thou* (p. viii). Williams might find insufficient warmth in the conception of identification as "a mental and moral act, involving intelligence and will . . ." This author carries his idea further than I am prepared to go, when he speaks of the coinherence of matter and deity in transubstantiation, which for him is the high point of coinherence (p. 115). This I reject, as do Reformed thinkers generally. Matter is at remote remove from personality, so that if there is an intimate interflow of deity and matter, and if anyone calls this phenomenon coinherence he is welcome; only it shows that coinherence is not the same thing as identification, which is personal in every form.

John McLeod Campbell has been set up and knocked down in many a textbook for nearly a century, but has been of influence on various modern thinkers such as Moberly and Vincent Taylor. Campbell's alleged heresy was vicarious repentance. This he repudiated; and R. C. Moberly (*Atonement and Personality*, Longmans, Green 1901), E. G. Bewkes (*Legacy of a Christian Mind*, Judson Press 1937), and V. Taylor (*The Cross of Christ*, Macmillan 1956, p. 96) agree that this was not Campbell's intention. Taylor says he did not mean a substitute repentance, but a spiritual offering with which we are to identify ourselves. The only point here is that in his major book, *The Nature of the Atonement* (London, Macmillan, 6th ed., 1886), without using the word, Campbell described the thing, identification. "Every time we are enabled, in spirit and in truth, through participation in the spirit of Christ, to confess sin before God, and meet His mind towards sin with such a response as . . . we are enabled to give, we have a clearer glimpse of the excellence of Christ's expiatory confession of our sins, and of the righteousness of God in accepting it on our behalf, to the end that we might thus share in it" (p. 288). True atonement he defines as "the feelings of the divine mind as to sin, being *present in humanity* [italics ours] and uttering themselves to God as a living voice from humanity" (p. 123). Christ "has taken the nature, and become the brother of those whose sins He confesses before the Father"; at the same time saying Amen to the mind of the Father, Amen to the divine condemnation (pp. 126-127).

R. C. Moberly in his notable book (*op. cit.*) uses the same word we have been using, identification, and means virtually the same thing by it. He does not attempt to set up distinctions among its types. The title of his book indicates that he is discussing identification in only one sphere, as we have not done. A special feature of his representation is the possibility of a man's identification not with another person but with righteousness. This is inexact language; it might better be said that a man may identify himself with the frame and "set" of the mind of a righteous man—or rather of a righteous God. To be more exact, he may wish to look at God, himself, and the world in the way God himself would look. Thus Moberly's identification, while it seems to be of a person with a complex of qualities, is rather an identification of one actual personal mind with another (ideal) mind. At its highest level this identification with righteousness is "nothing less than a personal self-identification, in love, with the love, which is also the holiness, of God" (p. 73). Christ is a divine Person, not so much God *and* man as God in, through, and as man; expressing himself in terms of humanity, making humanity, to the limits of possibility, a real and true reflection and utterance of deity. The central problem for Moberly is *forgiveness,* and this is effected by perfect penitence (not substitutionary repentance). "Perfect penitence would involve . . . a perfect re-identification of . . . the whole personality . . . with righteousness" (p. 117), which

on the negative side means penitence. Pardon is "that Divine acceptance . . . of the first divinely enabled identification of the
personality with any movement towards penitence" (p. 60). The
identification of Christ with the sinner is not complete in itself.
For the reality of our own relationship to the Atonement, "everything . . . turns upon the reality of *our identification, in spirit, with
the Spirit of Jesus Christ*" (p. 283, italics ours). Identification is
more than insight; Christ made himself one with man, one in
nature, one in love, himself humanity.

At the end of his moving book, Moberly dwells on the imperfection of all human identifications. He would agree with
Charles Williams that there is "no lovingness, mortal or divine,
which does not, for its mutual quality, depend on that sacrifice
[by Christ] of Himself." "By that central substitution . . . He
became everywhere the centre of, and everywhere He energized
and re-affirmed, all our substitutions and exchanges" (Symposium,
What the Cross Means to Me, James Clarke 1943, pp. 176 and
175). So, Moberly concludes, it will comfort us less, in our
moments of weakness or dying, to be adjured to remember the
dignity of our being, than to be pointed to the Cross. An emotional theology? Well . . . analyses may be cold, and should be;
but who can be cold in the presence of Reality?

I   *Notes and Acknowledgments*

1. *Make-Believe, Human and Divine*

1. C. E. M. Joad, *Guide to Philosophy* (New York: Dover Publications, 1946), Ch. XVI.

2. A great deal of literature has been written on this problem. See, e.g., A. J. Ayer (ed.), *Logical Positivism* (Glencoe, Ill.: The Free Press, 1958); Stuart Chase, *The Tyranny of Words* (New York: Harcourt, Brace & Company, 1938); Samuel I. Hayakawa, *Language in Action* (New York: Harcourt, Brace & Company, 1941). The preceding are more or less unwilling to ascribe meaning to theological language. More favorable are: Ian T. Ramsey, *Religious Language* (London: SCM Press Ltd., 1957); John Wilson, *Language and Christian Belief* (New York: St. Martin's Press, 1958); James Barr, *The Semantics of Biblical Language* (London: Oxford University Press, 1961).

3. John Calvin, *Institutes of the Christian Religion*, I. XIII. xxi.

4. A view persuasively expounded by Richard Kroner, *The Religious Function of Imagination* (New Haven: Yale University Press, 1941). E.g.: "Imagination is, as it were, more akin to the ultimate essence of life and reality than are thought and speculation" (p. 3). "Religious imagination is possible without revelation; but revelation is not possible without religious imagination" (p. 47).

5. Edward A. Dowey, Jr., *The Knowledge of God in Calvin's Theology* (New York: Columbia University Press, 1952), pp. 3-17.

6. Paul Tillich, *Systematic Theology* (Chicago: The University of Chicago Press, 1951), Vol. I, pp. 238-239.

7. Emil Brunner, *The Mediator*, tr. by Olive Wyon (Philadelphia: The Westminster Press, 1947), pp. 377-396. Especially pp. 386ff.: "The Christian 'myth' is that form of thought in which time is taken absolutely seriously; hence it is the only type of thought in which God is regarded as truly personal." Also p. 392: "He [God] Himself originated this 'myth.'" "This is His word; it is no human invention."

8. Austin Farrer, *The Glass of Vision* (London: Dacre Press, 1948), Lecture III.

9. See chapter 1, pp. 26-27.

10. See the classic passage in Augustine's *Confessions. The Confessions of St. Augustine,* tr. by J. G. Pilkington (New York: Liveright Publishing Corp., 1942), Book 10, Chs. VIII-XXI.

11. Perhaps some would agree that we have exactly the opposite situation with the devil. Satan also makes himself known; but always as a deceiver. He can put up a very good imitation, we are told, of an angel of light, though still the prince of darkness. Satan, as he wants (for the present) to be known, is not the actual Satan nor anything like him. God as he wants to be known is continuous and consistent with the God who can never be fully known. Satan, as he wants to be known (and we too, alas!), is pure deceit; God as he wants to be known is pure truth, even if the fullness of truth lie hidden in the depths of eternity. " 'Tis only the splendor of light hideth Thee."

12. 1 Kings 22:19-23.

13. E.g., Nels F. S. Ferré, *The Christian Understanding of God* (New York: Harper & Brothers, 1951), pp. 93-96, 113-114.

2. Identity and Identification

1. Some variety in points of view, along with a certain unity, may be seen in the following: Erik H. Erikson, in his essay "The Problem of Ego Identity," in Maurice R. Stein, *et al.* (eds.), *Identity and Anxiety* (Glencoe, Ill.: The Free Press, 1960): "The term identity points to an individual's link with the unique values, fostered by a unique history of his people" (pp. 37-38). "The term identity expresses such a mutual relation in that it connotes both a persistent sameness within oneself (self-sameness) and a persistent sharing of some kind of essential character with others" (p. 38). "At one time . . . [identity] will appear to refer to a conscious *sense of individual identity;* at another, to an unconscious striving for a *continuity of personal character;* at a third, as a criterion for the silent doings of *ego synthesis;* and, finally, as a maintenance of an inner *solidarity* with a group's ideals and identity" (p. 38). "The term identity covers much of what has been called the self by a variety of workers, be it in the form of a self-concept (George H. Mead), a self-system (Harry S. Sullivan), or in that of fluctuating self-experiences described by Schilder, Federn, and others" (p. 73).

Anselm L. Strauss in *Mirrors and Masks: The Search for Identity* (Glencoe, Ill.: The Free Press, 1959) takes a sociological view. By identity he means relationships or membership; and therefore can say (p. 109) that identity changes throughout life, and "is never gained nor maintained once and for all" (quoting Erikson, "The Problem of Identity," in *Journal of American Psychoanalysis,* IV, 1956).

Allen Wheelis in *The Quest for Identity* (New York: W. W. Norton & Co., 1958, p. 19) defines identity as a coherent sense of self. This is almost my use of the term, except that his emphasis falls on the *sense* rather than the *self,* and proceeds to put into "identity" much that I should include in "personality." Rollo May indicates another perspective when he writes: "The experience of one's own identity, or becoming a person, is the sim-

plest experience in life even though at the same time the most profound."
Rollo May, *Man's Search for Himself* (New York: W. W. Norton & Company, 1953), p. 92.

Gordon W. Allport in *Becoming* (New Haven: Yale University Press, 1955) illumines the problem especially in the sections "The Proprium" and "Is the Concept of Self Necessary?" "In psychology we have a state of affairs where empiricists, finding that they have gone as far as possible with analytic tools and being dissatisfied with the product, resort as did their predecessors to some concept of self in order to represent, however inadequately, the coherence, unity, and purposiveness they know they have lost in their fragmentary representations" (p. 38). "They have reintroduced self and ego unashamedly and, as if to make up for lost time, have employed ancillary concepts such as *self-image, self-actualization, self-affirmation, phenomenal ego, ego-involvement, ego-striving,* and many other hyphenated elaborations which to experimental positivism still have a slight flavor of scientific obscenity" (p. 37).

2. No apologies are necessary for bringing up psychological angles of a theological problem. As will appear, identification in the sense that I intend has to do with the will; it has to do with attitudes; it has to do with the way man—and, humanly speaking, God—thinks. If it sounds more suitable to say "subjective" rather than "psychological," there should be no great objection.

3. Incidentally, that may be the reason why Tillich's theology lacks, for many persons, the Christian note and a Christian appeal: he recognizes identity, but only with the sure prospect of losing it. E.g., "Finitude means having no definite place; it means having to lose every place finally and, with it, to lose being itself." Paul Tillich, *Systematic Theology,* Vol. I, p. 195.

4. Walt Whitman, "Song of Myself," strophe 32, in *Leaves of Grass & Democratic Vistas,* Everyman's Library (New York: E. P. Dutton & Co., 1912). R. Jeffers, "Ante Mortem" in *Modern American Poetry,* edited by Louis Untermeyer (New York: Harcourt, Brace & Company, fifth revised edition, 1936), p. 404.

5. In *I and Thou,* pp. 84f., Buber rejects what he calls "doctrines of absorption." "All real living is meeting," he says elsewhere (*op. cit.,* p. 11) (but, we might add, not melting!). Martin Buber, *I and Thou,* trans. by R. Gregor Smith, second edition (New York: Charles Scribner's Sons, 1958).

6. From *Death of a Salesman* by Arthur Miller, Act One, p. 56. Copyright 1949 by Arthur Miller. Reprinted by permission of The Viking Press, Inc.

7. C. S. Lewis, *The Screwtape Letters* (New York: The Macmillan Company, 1943).

8. C. S. Lewis, *Perelandra* (New York: The Macmillan Company, 1944).

9. It may be noted in passing that identification is not the same as simple connection. If a man joins a faculty or a firm, it will be said that he has identified with one or the other. But this may not be identification in the sense we intend. For the man may have no love for the job and no

intention of staying. He, and we, may be aware that he is a square peg in a round hole, an ugly duckling, the huckleberry in the pan of milk. He is in the firm, not of it. Identification, in our sense, takes place when the man and the firm, the individual and the group, or the two individuals, are not only thought of together, in some kind of connection, but are thought of *in the same way*, with the same inner attitude.

10. George L. Prestige, *God in Patristic Thought* (London: S.P.C.K., 1952), Ch. XIV. Charles Williams, *The Descent of the Dove* (New York: Oxford University Press, 1939), p. 234 and elsewhere.

11. The use of the term "real" to denote an alleged connection or identification which does *not* correspond to fact, may seem unjustified. I use it in this way for brevity's sake, and also because it is consistent with our definition of identification as an act of the will linking two personal entities, in consequence of which act certain relations are sustained or broken by the identifier. It will be seen that this definition leaves room for falsity in the identification. The reality (as I use the term "real" here) is in the act of will. If the act takes place, there is an identification; if not, not. But the truth or validity of the identification is yet to be determined. If the reader still balks at this use of the word *real*, then the word *alleged* or *attempted* may be substituted. The alleging, or the attempting, can be real enough, and yet what is alleged may be false or what is attempted never achieved.

3. Some Unjustified Identifications

1. "The Father has a body of flesh and bones as tangible as man's; the Son also; but the Holy Ghost has not a body of flesh and bones . . ." *The Doctrine and Covenants of the Church of Jesus Christ of Latter-Day Saints* (Salt Lake City: The Church of Jesus Christ of Latter-Day Saints, 1921), Section 130: 22.

2. Nels F. S. Ferré speaks at some length of God's body; but it is clear that he does not mean this in any but a symbolic sense, and not at all in the manner of the Latter-Day Saints. Nels F. S. Ferré, *The Christian Understanding of God* (New York: Harper & Brothers, 1951), pp. 34ff.

3. "Mysticism is . . . the perfecting and crown of all theology: as theology *par excellence*." The Orthodox speak of "union with God" as, e.g., the Reformed do; but apparently mean more by it, as their use of the word *theosis, deification,* indicates. Vladimir Lossky speaks of the "deifying energy of God"; and of man's becoming a "god by grace"; though he says the deification of the creature will take place in its fullness only after the resurrection of the dead. Vladimir Lossky, *The Mystical Theology of the Eastern Church* (London: James Clarke & Co., 1957), pp. 9, 126, *et alibi saepe.*

4. There appears to be a lack of clarity on this point. Emile Mersch (following St. Athanasius with enthusiasm) speaks much of "deification"; and even of a "real, ontological union" between man and God, despite the church's protestations that the creature always remains creature, the finite finite. Emile Mersch, *The Whole Christ,* tr. by John R. Kelly, S.J. (Mil-

waukee: The Bruce Publishing Company, 1938). Mersch elsewhere, however, speaks of the union as "psychological." Emile Mersch, *The Theology of the Mystical Body,* tr. by Cyril Vollert, S.J. (St. Louis and London: B. Herder Book Co., 1951), p. 350. Here again he speaks of the Christian's life by divine adoption as "nothing less than a participation in the very filiation of the Son . . . participation in the Trinity" (p. 466).

5. Questions arise here as to the permissibility and validity of Hellenic elements in Christian theology, as contrasted with Hebraic; but that is aside from our point. Certainly if there is any doctrine in the church which is entirely Hellenic without a trace of Hebraic influence, it would be this.

6. "The speculative utterances of mysticism are always more or less pantheistic in character" (*Encyclopaedia Britannica,* 14th ed.; see Mysticism, p. 51). The ambiguous nature of mysticism, showing why it can be both attacked and defended as anti-Christian and Christian, can be illustrated by one of Meister Eckhart's recent translators. "We should notice that he [Eckhart] never fell victim to the illusion that 'I, this earthly individual, whom men call Brother Eckhart, am God.' Far from it . . . still, in spite of their endless differences, if God and man are of the same genus, it must be possible to set free the divine kernel of being in man's inmost self . . . This . . . 'little spark' of God which is concealed within the shell of selfhood . . . is the germ of eternal life and the seed of God." Raymond Bernard Blakney, *Meister Eckhart, A Modern Translation* (New York: Harper & Brothers, 1941; Torchbook paperback edition 1957), pp. xx-xxi.

7. Martin Buber, who is "mystical" enough, points out that John, most mystical of evangelists, gives no support to "absorptionism." "I and Thou are One" is not the same as "I am Thou and Thou art I." Martin Buber, *I and Thou,* tr. by R. Gregor Smith (New York: Charles Scribner's Sons, 1958); see pp. 84f.

8. Dionysius the Areopagite, *Mystical Theology,* as quoted in Charles Williams, *The Descent of the Dove* (London: The Religious Book Club, 1939), pp. 61-62.

9. "The term *souls* or *spirits* is as improper as the term *gods.* Soul or Spirit signifies Deity and nothing else. There is no finite soul nor spirit. Soul or Spirit means only one Mind." Further, "Mind is God," and "God, good, is the *only* Mind." Mary Baker Eddy, *Science and Health with Key to the Scriptures* (Boston: The First Church of Christ, Scientist, 1906), pp. 466, 469.

10. Roman Catholics, who generally do not appreciate to what an extent their church's attitude to Mary blocks understanding between them and the Protestant world, will protest against this interpretation, on two counts. For one thing, Mary reigns in heaven without a consort, and for another (as already noted) she is still a creature. The Protestant rejoinder would run like this: True, Mary has no consort. But that does not have much to do with the question: Why do you offer Mary, confessedly a creature, such honor as belongs to God alone? The ease with which she can be thought of as divine is shown in countries where the local goddess

has been replaced by the Virgin of Lima, the Virgin of Guadalupe, and so on.

11. Erwin R. Goodenough, *Religious Tradition and Myth* (New Haven: Yale University Press, 1937).

12. Ferré, *op. cit.*, p. 174. Mersch, *The Theology of the Mystical Body,* is full of the idea.

13. Lesslie Newbigin, *The Reunion of the Church* (London: SCM Press, 1948). Chapter on "The Extension of the Incarnation?", pp. 55f.

14. A. A. Hodge, *The Atonement* (Philadelphia: Presbyterian Board of Publication, 1867), Ch. VII.

15. John Murray, *The Imputation of Adam's Sin* (Grand Rapids: Wm. B. Eerdmans Publishing Co., 1959).

16. C. H. Dodd, *The Epistle of Paul to the Romans* (New York: Harper & Brothers, 1932), commentary on Romans 5:12-21. Emil Brunner, *The Christian Doctrine of Creation and Redemption* (Philadelphia: The Westminster Press, 1952), chapter 3.

17. Augustus H. Strong, *Systematic Theology,* Revised 1906 (Philadelphia: The Judson Press, 1912), p. 628.

18. Dr. Murray distinguishes between his view, which is that of the older Protestant scholastics, and that of Dr. Charles Hodge, which is a variation on it. According to Dr. Hodge, all that is imputed is the guilt which is defined as the "obligation to satisfy justice." "To impute sin . . . is to impute the guilt of sin. And by guilt is meant not criminality or moral ill-desert, or demerit, much less moral pollution, but the judicial obligation to satisfy justice." (Charles Hodge, *Systematic Theology,* Vol. II, p. 194; quoted by John Murray, *op. cit.*, p. 73.) Murray, dealing with John Owen's treatment of the problem, differs with Dr. Hodge's construction. "There can be no obligation to the penalty of sin [i.e., no obligation to satisfy justice] without the sin which is the proper ground of that obligation" (p. 79). Hence, in Dr. Murray's view, what was imputed was not only guilt but the sin on account of which the guilt was incurred. There are three Latin words which Dr. Murray prefers: *culpa, reatus,* and *poena* —sin, liable, and penalty. One who sins is liable (*reatus*) for the sin (*culpa*) and to penalty (*poena*). Murray lays great stress on the assertion that it must be the *sin* which is imputed, for there can be no *reatus* without *culpa*. In fact, he identifies *reatus culpae* with *reatus poenae.*

19. For some reason, it is always the first sin of Adam, exclusively, which is in view in this theory of imputation. John Murray lays great stress on the point.

20. A. A. Hodge, *Outlines of Theology,* Edition of 1878 (Grand Rapids: Wm. B. Eerdmans Publishing Company, 1928), p. 359.

21. Charles Hodge, *Systematic Theology* (New York: Charles Scribner's Sons, 1909), Vol. II, p. 196.

22. L. Berkhof, *Systematic Theology* (Grand Rapids: Wm. B. Eerdmans Publishing Company, 1941), p. 213.

23. Cf. George S. Hendry, commenting on the Westminster Confession of Faith, VII. 2. *The Westminster Confession for Today* (Richmond, Va.: John Knox Press, 1960).

24. The Augustinian or You-were-there theory of the transmission of sin does claim that in a real sense each one of us *was* Adam, or that he was each of us; but as Dr. Murray carefully points out, that is not the metaphysic back of the imputation theology.

25. Dr. Murray seeks to find an expression which will on the one hand admit the fact that (in his words) "the individual members of the race did not *personally* and *individually* participate in the sin of this human nature as it existed in its unity in Adam" (*op. cit.*, p. 32), and on the other hand defend the proposition that "the sin of Adam is reckoned by God as the sin also of posterity." How can we say that disobedience is imputed (which Murray does say, p. 88) if we did not disobey, personally and individually? Dr. Murray finds the key word to be "property"; we have a property in Adam's disobedience, and this property is defined as "participation in the *culpa* of his transgression" (p. 88). In short, having a property in the disobedience means that while we were not personally disobedient, and did not share in the disobedience, we do share in the sin of the disobedience. By such devious verbal devices is the doctrine upheld.

26. It should be noted that on this theory the word *covenant* is used almost as a synonym for *commandment*, the difference being that covenant involves a promise, commandment does not. Strong, *op. cit.*, p. 613.

27. Murray would add: the sin of the act.

28. As quoted by Strong, *op. cit.*, p. 615.

29. That the curse is laid on the whole race does not prevent the conclusion that every baby born is born personally cursed, and that the guilt is imputed immediately, not mediately.

30. A. A. Hodge, *Outlines of Theology* (1878), p. 358.

4. Identification in the Heart of God

1. See, e.g., L. Berkhof, *Systematic Theology* (Grand Rapids: Wm. B. Eerdmans Publishing Company, 1941); also R. Garrigou-Lagrange, *God: His Existence and Nature,* tr. by Dom Bede Rose, Vol. II, p. 172, refers to the baptismal formula as "incomprehensible" (St. Louis and London: B. Herder Book Co., 1936; sixth printing, 1955). Augustine, *On the Trinity,* XV. 23. 44; also XV. 27. 50, in *Nicene and Post-Nicene Fathers,* edited by Philip Schaff (New York: Charles Scribner's Sons, 1886-1889, 1917); Edward A. Dowey, Jr., *The Knowledge of God in Calvin's Theology* (New York: Columbia University Press, 1952), pp. 3-6, with references there.

John Calvin writes with approval: "Hilary accuses the heretics of a great crime, in constraining him . . . to expose to the danger of human language those things which ought to be confined within the religion of the mind . . . This is to . . . express things inexpressible . . . Very similar is the excuse of Augustine, that this word [Trinity] was extorted by necessity . . . not for the sake of expressing what God is, but to avoid passing it over in total silence." John Calvin, *The Institutes of the Christian Religion,* tr. by John Allen (Philadelphia: Presbyterian Board of Publication, 1841), I. XIII. v.

2. *Institutes of the Christian Religion,* I. XIII. xvii.

3. Benjamin B. Warfield, *The Lord of Glory* (New York: American Tract Society, 1907); Saint Athanasius, *Letters Concerning the Holy Spirit*, tr. by C. R. B. Shapland (London: Epworth Press, 1951). It should be said, by the way, that Warfield's book "proves too much," while Athanasius is much better at defending the deity of the Spirit than at demonstrating the unity of the Spirit with Father and Son.

4. 2 Corinthians 5:10; Romans 14:10.

5. Romans 8:35, 39.

6. Romans 5:5; Ephesians 3:17; Romans 8:16.

7. Herman Bavinck, *The Doctrine of God*, tr. by William Hendriksen (Grand Rapids: Wm. B. Eerdmans Publishing Company, 1951), p. 303. "Father, Son, and Spirit . . . have distinct personal properties . . . the distinctness of the persons is completely expressed by the so-called 'personal attributes or properties'; viz. '(a) paternity or fatherhood, innascibility or unbegottenness, active generation, active spiration; (b) filiation or sonship, passive generation, active spiration; and (c) procession or passive spiration.'" Edward Arthur Litton, *Introduction to Dogmatic Theology*, new edition, edited by Philip E. Hughes (London: James Clarke & Co., Ltd., 1960), pages 99-105, presents this at some length.

8. Three quite different books on the Trinity may be named. Claude Welch, *In This Name* (New York: Charles Scribner's Sons, 1952); Leonard Hodgson, *The Doctrine of the Trinity* (New York: Charles Scribner's Sons, 1944); Cyril Charles Richardson, *The Doctrine of the Trinity* (Nashville: Abingdon Press, 1958). Welch surveys various contemporary expositions of the Trinity, notably Barth's. Hodgson presents a "societal" view of the Trinity, opposite to that of Barth. Richardson criticizes the doctrine root and branch.

Of course this is included in all comprehensive books of dogmatic theology, Karl Barth's extensive treatment being currently the most famous. Karl Barth, *Church Dogmatics*, English translation by G. T. Thomson (Edinburgh: T. & T. Clark, 1936), Vol. I, Part I, Ch. II, pp. 339-560.

9. Garrigou-Lagrange, *op. cit.*, Vol. I, pp. 295f. A typical Thomist defense of the concept.

10. A different view is taken by George L. Prestige, *God in Patristic Thought* (London: S. P. C. K., 1952). "The more observant and profound of Western theologians recognised the characteristic meaning of the Greek doctrine to be that of 'three Objects,' and not 'three Subjects'" (pp. 240-241). "The psychological centre of God is to be sought in the ousia rather than in the Persons" (p. 284). "The result of the extended theological process (of the early Christian centuries) may be summed up . . . in the formula that in God there are three divine organs of God-consciousness, but one centre of divine self-consciousness. As seen and thought, He is three; as seeing and thinking, He is one" (p. 301). Hodgson (*op. cit.*) leans more toward tritheism in saying that the evidence "requires us to believe in a God whose unity unifies three activities each of which is made known to us as a distinct Person in the full sense of that word. Each is a He, none is an it" (p. 140).

11. See 1 Corinthians 15:28 (K.J.V.).

12. This is the spirit of Augustine's *Treatise on the Trinity* throughout, especially Book XV. Hodgson (*op. cit.*) connects Trinitarian thinking with "Trinitarian religion," apart from which it is not likely that the doctrine of the Trinity will have a living meaning (p. 177). A weak spot in Augustine's presentation is his hypostatizing (as the Spirit) the love between the divine Father and Son. Tentative with Augustine, this has been unequivocally emphasized by some Christians since. C. S. Lewis, *Mere Christianity* (New York: The Macmillan Company, 1958), p. 136: "The union between the Father and Son is such a live concrete thing that this union itself is also a Person." Surely it is better to say that the love is *in* each person, not something like a connecting line between them.

13. The mode of being which the Creator possesses differs so radically from the mode of being of any created thing or person that one is not greatly surprised at Tillich's denial that the term *exist*, positively or negatively, has any application to God. The Christian does insist, however, that God IS, though the use of the words "exist" and "existence" in these pages must not be taken as a claim that God and his creatures exist in the same way.

14. "What a horrible curse we have deserved, seeing all the harmless creatures from earth to heaven have suffered punishment for our sins; for in that they labour under corruption, that cometh to pass through our fault." John Calvin, *Commentary on Romans 8:21.* Tr. by Christopher Rosdell (Edinburgh: The Calvin Translation Society, 1844). Reinhold Niebuhr comments in this connection: "It can hardly be denied that the Pauline authority, supporting the idea that physical death is a consequence of sin, introduced a note into Christian theology which is not fully in accord with the total Biblical view of the finiteness of man." Reinhold Niebuhr, *The Nature and Destiny of Man* (New York: Charles Scribner's Sons, 1945), Vol. I, p. 176.

15. See, e.g., E. L. Mascall, *Christian Theology and Natural Science* (New York: Longmans, Green & Co., 1956), ch. 4.

16. A book on this theme has a similar title: L. P. Jacks, *My Neighbor the Universe* (New York: G. P. Putnam's Sons, 1929).

17. John Dewey's Terry Lectures are a fair presentation of religion without a theistic God. John Dewey, *A Common Faith* (New Haven: Yale University Press, 1934).

18. Emil Brunner, *Man in Revolt*, tr. by Olive Wyon (London: Lutterworth Press, 1939; Philadelphia: The Westminster Press, 1947), p. 99. "The intrinsic worth of man's being lies in the Word of God, hence his nature is: responsibility from love, in love, for love." As Cairns expounds Brunner, the image of God, *formally*, is not lost; for man, whether he sins or not, is a subject of God and therefore responsible. Materially, however, the image is completely lost, since man is a sinner in total depravity. David Cairns, *The Image of God in Man* (London: SCM Press, Ltd., 1953). One cannot quarrel with Brunner over the great importance and uniqueness of man's responsibility before God; but it is questionable whether this is the Biblical meaning of the "image of God."

19. If any evidence were needed, consider the hard sledding the prin-

ciple of stewardship has in the churches. Yet stewardship is simply the practical carrying out of the principle of identification with the aims of God. Many church members seem to suppose that identification is sufficient if one hears about what God is doing, approves of it, and sings about it.

20. "[Man] belongs to the same order of being as God Himself . . . If we were not like God, we could not know Him." Charles Hodge, *Systematic Theology* (New York: Charles Scribner's Sons, 1909), Vol. II, p. 97.

21. II Esdras 6:56. *The Apocrypha:* An American Translation, by Edgar J. Goodspeed (Chicago: The University Press, 1938).

22. For an extended discussion of the suffering of God and man, see H. Wheeler Robinson, *Suffering, Human and Divine* (New York: The Macmillan Company, 1939). For a historical survey, with comment, see John Kenneth Mozley, *The Impassibility of God* (Cambridge: The University Press, 1926).

5. *The Identifications of Christ*

1. There seems to be a very widespread dissatisfaction, among Protestant theologians, with the formulas of Chalcedon, as using the categories of neo-Platonism (or Middle Platonism as Pittenger prefers). A distinction must be made, however, between those theologians who, while desiring to discard the formulas, also wish to discard the faith the formulas were designed to define; and those who would discard the formulas on the ground of present meaninglessness, but search for other formulas, in categories of present-day thinking, to express for our time what the Chalcedonian document expressed for its time. An example of the former is an article by W. O. Johnson, "The Coming Copernican Christology," in *The Hibbert Journal* for October 1960. An example of the latter is W. Norman Pittenger, *The Word Incarnate* (New York: Harper & Brothers, 1959).

Of course, the "Catholic" scholar speaks of the "sacred formulas" of Chalcedon. But to a Protestant no formula is sacred.

2. George Meredith, "Lucifer in Starlight," in *The Oxford Book of English Verse,* new edition (Oxford: Oxford University Press, 1939), p. 960.

3. Cf. Alfred E. Garvie, *The Christian Faith* (New York: Charles Scribner's Sons, 1937), p. 149: "We must not lapse into tritheism and represent the Incarnation as the manifestation and activity of the Son alone. God in His wholeness and fullness participated in the Incarnation. We are here not concerned with *static natures,* but with *dynamic presence."* This seems also to be the drift of Donald Baillie, *God Was in Christ* (New York: Charles Scribner's Sons, 1948), Ch. VI.

4. This is George S. Hendry's thesis in his *Gospel of the Incarnation.* E.g., p. 31: "The severance between incarnation and atonement is the result of a failure to grasp the link that connects them, viz., the historical life of the incarnate Christ." George S. Hendry, *The Gospel of the Incarnation* (Philadelphia: The Westminster Press, 1958).

5. This is not to say that all its features as historically developed are defensible or in harmony with the New Testament. It is to say that it is

true that Christ in some sense stood in our stead, took our place, and that this substitution lies at the heart of the Atonement.

6. Berkhof lays down rules for what is legal and what is not, as if he were the consulting jurist for the celestial court. L. Berkhof, *Systematic Theology* (Grand Rapids: Wm. B. Eerdmans Publishing Company, 1941), p. 376.

7. Robert S. Paul, *The Atonement and the Sacraments* (Nashville: Abingdon Press, 1960), p. 119.

8. James Denney, *The Atonement and the Modern Mind* (London: Hodder and Stoughton, 1903), p. 46; quoted in Paul, *op. cit.*, p. 215.

9. E.g., W. Kolfhaus, *Christusgemeinschaft bei Johannes Calvin.* Buchhandlung des Erziehungsvereins Neukirchen, Kr. Moers 1939. "Justification is for John Calvin the act of God in which he gives himself to us and gives Christ, with whom we are united in Christ into one body" (p. 61). "The forgiveness of sins is not the cold sentence of a judge but an act springing from love, an act which sets us in community" (p. 62). (This from a man who—Kolfhaus says—"never forgot the forensic point of view for a moment" [p. 64]. Kolfhaus quotes Martin Kähler: "The life and essence of Christianity is present only where there is living communion with Christ" (p. 150). (My translation of Kolfhaus here and elsewhere.)

H. Wheeler Robinson, *Redemption and Revelation* (New York: Harper & Brothers, 1942): "The truth of retribution is not denied, if God Himself shares in the suffering which it entails. . . . His loving acceptance of . . . [suffering through our sins] transforms it into grace, and removes the final obstacle to forgiveness. . . . The words of God [words of pardon] come not as a superficial and arbitrary discharge from condemnation; they are spoken by One who knows the cost of forgiveness in the suffering which the sin has brought upon Himself, as upon the crucified Redeemer" (p. 274).

10. See a little-read classic: John McLeod Campbell, *The Nature of the Atonement* (London: James Clarke & Co., Ltd., 1959; quotations are from the 1873 edition of Macmillan and Co.). Campbell repudiates the term "vicarious repentance," thinking rather of Christ as offering the perfect contrition, the perfect renunciation of sin. Yet this seems only a few shades removed from the idea of a vicarious offering. This, Campbell feels, is the "equivalent sorrow and repentance" for which Jonathan Edwards sought a place (Ch. VI, p. 123). Christ offers what man cannot offer (p. 125). This construction is usually brushed off as morally impossible and immoral if it were possible. But is it morally impossible in the light of the principle of identification? And is the transfer, or the imputation, of repentance any less moral than the transfer of guilt, from person to person?

11. Some Reformed theologians would regard this as much too broad a view of the matter. Motivated in part by unwillingness to think of Christ's sacrifice as in the slightest degree misdirected or wasted, they affirm that Christ willed to be one only with a selected number. Their quarrel would be not with the principle of identification as such, but with the scope of it envisaged here.

12. *The Westminster Shorter Catechism*, Question 21.

13. See Alice Meynell's poem, "Christ in the Universe," *The Catholic Anthology* (New York: The Macmillan Company, 1943), p. 319.

14. See chapter 3, pp. 58-59.

15. Kolfhaus (*op. cit.*) carefully distinguishes for himself and for Calvin between "Christ-Mysticism" and the view which Calvin held. The basic element of mysticism is a striving of man for immediate communion with God, for a sinking into the Godhead, the "de-becoming" (*Entwerden*) of man, being taken up into God . . . None of this belongs to the genuine Christian point of view as Calvin sees it (p. 126).

6. *The Identifications of a Christian*

1. John McLeod Campbell, *The Nature of the Atonement*, p. 16: Atonement follows forgiveness. (London: Macmillan and Co., 1873.) Also Vincent Taylor, *Forgiveness and Reconciliation*, p. 10, defines forgiveness as the canceling of obstacles to reconciliation. (London: Macmillan and Co., Ltd., 1941.)

2. McLeod Campbell says: ". . . Christ, the holy one of God, bearing the sins of all men on His spirit—in Luther's words, 'the one sinner'—and meeting the cry of these sins for judgment, and the wrath due to them, absorbing and exhausting that divine wrath in that adequate confession and perfect response on the part of man, which was possible only to the infinite and eternal righteousness in humanity" (*op. cit.*, p. 125).

3. "Forgiveness is not a transaction which can be taken by itself and stated as it were in terms of arithmetic. It is an attitude of a person to a person. It can only be understood in terms of personality." R. C. Moberly, *Atonement and Personality* (New York: Longmans, Green and Co., 1910), p. 54. See also Vincent Taylor's comments in his *Forgiveness and Reconciliation*, Ch. I. He points out a "wide difference between the meaning of forgiveness in the New Testament and its significance in modern theology. Whereas in the former it denotes the removal of the barriers to reconciliation, in the latter it signifies full restoration to fellowship" (pp. 27-28).

4. See, e.g., Principal Caird as quoted in Thomas Hywel Hughes, *The Atonement* (London: George Allen & Unwin, Ltd., 1949), p. 240.

5. A. A. Hodge, *op. cit.*, p. 369: "It is a vicarious penal satisfaction, which can be admitted in any case only at the arbitrary discretion of the sovereign."

6. See McLeod Campbell, *op. cit.*, p. 288.

7. James Denney, *The Christian Doctrine of Reconciliation*, pp. 96-100; quoted in T. H. Hughes, *op. cit.*, p. 85.

8. There are at least three meanings intended by the Greek back of the English word "sanctification" in the New Testament. It is sometimes a synonym for dedication or consecration, the condition of being set apart for special service to God, or for a special kind of life, as all Christians are. Sometimes it has a proleptic use, an apparent fiction, like justification and forgiveness. People who are far from perfect, far indeed from ordinary standards of decency, are called—startlingly to us and no doubt to them —sanctified. Eventually they will be made perfect, but Paul may use the

word as if they were already lacking in nothing. Sometimes, again, the word means what it means in the Westminster Standards, a "work of God's free grace, whereby we are renewed in the whole man after the image of God, and are enabled more and more to die unto sin, and live unto righteousness" (Shorter Catechism, Q. 35). This third usage is the one intended here.

9. No attempt is made here to set forth even in outline a doctrine of the Spirit, only to note certain points where the principle of identification comes into sight. R. C. Moberly is especially helpful here. For example: "The hope of forgiveness merely, which is not, of inherent necessity, the hope of a heart set on righteousness,—is a pagan rather than a Christian hope. . . . [Even the dying tears of those who have failed] may yet be, in them, a real beginning of capacity . . . of what, in its full development, will become nothing less than a personal self-identification, in love, with the love, which is also the holiness, of God" (*op. cit.*, pp. 72-73).

Again: "The Spirit of the Incarnate in us is not only our personal association, but our personal union, with the Incarnate Christ. . . . He is . . . our own personal response. . . . He is Christ Himself in us" (p. 204).

"For the reality of our own relation to the atonement . . . everything unreservedly turns upon the *reality of our identification, in spirit, with the Spirit of Jesus Christ*" (p. 283). (Italics ours.)

10. For a stimulating study of the Holy Spirit, approaching from the human side, see Arnold B. Come, *Human Spirit and Holy Spirit* (Philadelphia: The Westminster Press, 1959).

11. D. M. Baillie, *God Was in Christ* (New York: Charles Scribner's Sons, 1948), Ch. V.

12. For a clear exposition of the difference, see Kolfhaus, *Christusgemeinschaft bei Johannes Calvin*, ch. 8 (Buchhandlung des Erziehungsvereins Neukirchen, Kr. Moers, 1939).

13. L'Abbé Nédoncelle, *La Réciprocité des Consciences*, pp. 71ff.; quoted in Martin Jarrett-Kerr, *The Hope of Glory: The Atonement in Our Time* (London: SCM Press, Ltd., 1952), pp. 93-94.

14. See John Calvin, *The Institutes of the Christian Religion*, III. VII. vi.

15. The word "sister" is seldom found. It is often implied; but the difficulty which even Apostles had with thinking of women as primary members with the same status as men has continued to the present day, and illustrates how common mores limit and shape or misshape Christian ideals.

16. Author unknown.